A NEV ANOTHER CHANCE

MARI HODGES

About the author.....

Every page in this book has been inspired by events and people in my own personal life. There are so many people that play a part in my life, far too many to name, but each have left a foot print upon my heart. In fact many times I am also inspired by the people around me that I don't even know. I send my love and gratitude to all of you. You know who you are.

Then of course there are those people in your life that have such a tremendous impact on your life that you are forever changed. I'd like to start by thanking my family because I know that they were hand selected, each and every one by God to remind me how to love.

My son Curtis, the laid back young man that has the gentlest heart and the greatest gift of music has taught me the biggest lessons of unconditional love. He is the oldest child, so as most of you know those babies don't come with instructions. I'm pretty sure I was not qualified for that job when I signed up. Thank God for "on the job" training. One of my favorite sayings has always been "God doesn't call the qualified, he qualifies the called".

Then came my youngest child, my daughter Danielle. She is a remarkable young lady, her high energy and enthusiasm always amazes me. She is a very dedicated and determined young woman whose personality shines brighter than the sun. I have come to realize over the years that these two children I thought I was raising were in fact raising me. My children were opposite in so many ways that it created the most amazing opportunities to learn how to really love others, but more importantly it taught me how to love myself. It occurred to me that if I split myself in half, all my qualities and behaviors you'd have them. These children were the perfect balance and combination of me. My love for them helped me to learn to accept the parts I didn't like or understand, and how to forgive people when they were really only doing what they knew how to do. It had never occurred to me before that most people are really doing the best they know how to do.

I also want to thank my daughter in law Brittany. Her love for my son has been such a blessing. While many times have been challenging, these two have been able to grow closer and remember always how to come back to the love that brought them together in the first place. They have given me one of the most precious gifts and that is my grandson Tripp. He is an angel sent straight from God. They say Gods timing is perfect and as much as we may question it, ultimately we all know that it is true.

My biggest teacher and supporter was always my mom, Kathy. The role of a mother cannot be described in words but it can be felt on the deepest levels of your very being. My mom was my best friend. She saw things in me that I never understood until I had my own children. On those days when I felt like life would just eat me up and swallow me whole, I'd pick up the phone and she would always remind me how amazing I was. For many years I'd tell her "your just saying that because you're my mom and you have to" which is funny for those of you that knew my mom would remember that she always said exactly what was on her mind in a no nonsense kind of way and she never "HAD" to say anything. When I started this book I'd call her everyday to read it to her and for the first two weeks she didn't realize that I was the one writing it. My cover was blown one day when she requested that I read ahead a day. After a brief argument about why I couldn't read a day ahead she wanted a logical reason and not all the excuses I had given, so I simply stated that I had not written it yet. I wanted an unbiased opinion of the book and she thought it was just another inspirational gem that I was introducing her to. Those are the moments that make a mother proud. She wasn't surprised at all, but she was so amazed that I was going to do this. That's when I knew she had been right all those years about me having a great gift. I wasn't great at singing, dancing or any of the other things that I thought meant you had a gift. I always wanted to be prettier or smarter or more popular, good at what everyone else seemed to be good at. I was always different. Then I started working in a specialty baby retail store over 23 years ago and I realized the gifts I had were just as different. I had the ability to relate to others, I found people very fascinating. I love helping others and God gave me the gift of words, not only in writing but in speaking. I have a career that has given me the opportunity to not only help people but to actually save lives and to educate others to save lives as well. In learning to help others save lives I also learned how to save my own.

During the course of writing this book, I lost someone very special to me by suicide. My family was devastated. I would call my mom sobbing in tears, often times unable to control myself. She would say "Stop crying for what you think you are missing out on and be grateful for the times that you had with Mark, because that man truly loved you, he just didn't know how to love himself enough and he was ready to go home" It wasn't easy but she was right once again. I began to try to find something positive in the devastation of his death and remind myself that God was still very much at work in my life. It would be several years before I would understand the gift that Mark had given to me and my family not only in his life, but also in his death. I thought that I was close to God and that I understood many things but as you read this book and see my heart poured out onto paper you will notice that these events in my life actually allowed me to truly know myself as I learned to know God, God as I understood him. Something my mom and Mark had in common other than me was that they were both recovering alcoholics. I have the most respect for the lessons that their lives brought to me and all the lives that they touched because I could see that no matter what you may have done or been through it all happens for a reason and that you are never alone regardless of how it looks. My mom held my hand once again as I learned to work through another crisis in my life, one that I didn't believe I would recover from. Then my mom was diagnosed with cancer the Christmas before my 39th birthday. She went home just days after the following Valentine's day. Our time together in those final days was so amazing, for while my heart was ripping out once again, it was also at such peace because she was so excited to go home. My mom had the most amazing faith of any person I have ever known and I was very blessed to have had such a fabulous example of what is possible when you believe. The life that she lived was a very difficult path for all of us, but she found happiness, love and knew who she was and where she was going. The morning she died I sat outside her hospital room on the floor crying once again feeling like I would never be able to quit, and then I heard her voice, very loud and clear "Stop crying for what you think you are missing out on and be grateful for the time we had, because I truly love you." I knew right then the gift that Mark had given to me. For had I not experienced his death I would not have been able to survive the loss of my mom.

For almost a year I was so devastated that I couldn't write at all. I still pick up the phone to call her. Before my mom died she said that God had something so amazing in store for me and that I would understand soon, that the love of my life was out there and now I'd finally be ready for him. She'd say "I didn't find my Wessie until I was 40 and so will you". That was the last thing on my mind but that's what moms do, they keep us inspired so we don't give up. My mom knew I was happy on my own, and that my walls had been built so high that I was too busy to let someone in. I was too independent to go through all that again and she knew that it would really have to be obvious to me that God had a plan with this guy because it had become real easy to walk away. God would need to send someone that was impossible for me to walk away from, someone that I couldn't use all my great *"cut and run because it is hard"* patterns on, someone that I was willing to see with my heart and not only my head.

Then on New Years of 2010 I met up after 23 years with one of my favorite childhood friends. Our families had been close and my mom always adored this kid. My first Valentine card, candies and flowers were given to me by him. I clearly remember my mom explaining how much effort someone would go to at that age to buy a young lady a valentine. I still have that card. When I saw my friend David I knew instantly that my mom had been talking about him. It's almost as if a team of angels and my mother coordinated our paths back together. God really is smart because this is one of the few people in this world that I genuinely loved before I went out into the world and got hurt. We spent hours as kids trying to learn to moon walk, and just hang out trying to survive the crazy families we were being raised by. David's life had been very rough as a boy and I would just cry to my mom about it. She would say he is going to grow up and be an honorable man because he is a warrior, he is tough but he has a gentle heart, God will take care of him you will see. David has inspired me in ways that I can't even find words for. This was one of my best friends and I loved him in the fourth grade, before I knew what that even meant. Feeling a love like this when I was sure that my heart had been so broken that I couldn't possibly feel anything again was truly a gift from God. I was able to pick up the pen and finish the book. My life is such an unpredictable journey of not only tragedy but of the most amazing triumph. I am so grateful to everyone and above all to God for the constant unconditional love provided to me through so many people and in so many ways. I don't know where life will take me next but what I do know is that I am not alone. We are all in this together.

Special thanks and love to: My family, My dad Wes, thank you for finally finding my mom and giving her the best 26 years of her life. She deserved you!! Aunt Mary & Uncle Ken, I'd need another book to tell you what you guys mean to me, my many cousins especially the Kite kids, you all were my siblings, Aunt Fran & Uncle Bob, this is what a story book marriage would look like I finally found my "Uncle Bob". My sister Penny, (Dani Lee) we couldn't even begin to make up a story that is as fascinating as ours really is!, My bro John- I'm so proud of you and so was mom, finally you are the BIG brother, My sister Joyce-you know I love you and I know you will get to where you are going in life, that green butterfly is a reminder! My sister Tina, we gotta take care of your daddy now, we were raised together so you know you got it in you to make it through the hard parts. You are a warrior angel lil sister don't forget that! All my other family members you are in my heart thank you.

My friends (the selected family): Harris J. there aren't enough words to thank you for the role you play in our life, my mom would be so grateful to you, you are one of my bff. Terri S. I have learned so many things from our friendship; I'm so proud of you and love you dearly. Gotta love those boys of ours! Dave H, you know how I feel, our friendship is truly a gift. Danny H, thank you for one of the most amazing gifts in my life, our daughter, I simply adore her. I would do it all again. No regrets. Roy O, I learned true forgiveness from you, thank you for the most fabulous son. I miss you every day. Mike L, what an adventure you have been in my life, what could I possibly say. You already know. Kristi T, I love you, thanks for always being there even when I didn't think I needed anyone. Tracy C, you will always have a special place in my heart, you know the pages you have inspired in this book and I will always be grateful for our friendship. Just look at the title. Buffalo Moon community- I have been so blessed to be a part of such an amazing community. I have such a respect for the Native ways and I am forever grateful to Joseph Rael, Neil and Elizabeth for opening up their hearts and ways for this girl to understand the red their hearts and ways for this girl to understand the red road heart that beats within her, my years of dancing taught me more about life than I could ever explain. I love each and every person that is part of that community or has ever been or will ever be. My love and thanks to the CPST world, you know who you are, I have been honored to work in the fields saving lives with each and every one of you. Together we have really made a difference. When I'm outside in 110 degree weather checking a car seat I understand that this is just one of those ways we have all been called to serve, the Safe kids soldiers, I am forever inspired by you all. My Baby's 1st family, I love you all and am very honored to represent a business and family that genuinely does things for the same reasons I do, that is how it should be. Greg D, my book partner, I love you more than I could possibly say. Thank you for always being there for me when I thought I was too broken to have one word to say, when I didn't feel like anyone would really care about anything I had to say, since my life looked like a train wreck, your positive outlook and spectacular ways have made this book a reality. The first of many, so keep that camera handy! I'm jealous though so expect me to be on some of those trips with you and Tamara.

You all know the parts you have played for me. Muah Muah I love you ALL!!

About the photographer.....

The imagery in this book was made possible by my parents who gave me the opportunity to get degrees in photography and industrial design no matter how long it took; the great opportunities I have been given to travel around this spectacular country mostly via motorcycle; all the wonderful people in my life that continue to inspire me especially Wendy Franklin, Mark Steel, John Amato, Stacey Bundren, Deborah Going, Jim Ross, Mari Hodges, Boston Jim, Mark Walkingstick, Pat Fogerty, Ann Luckett, and of course my other half Tamara Heye soon to be Desmond.

May you find some peace, pleasure, and meaning in the images that follow...

Enjoy the ride today.. I will..

Greg Desmond

D edication…..

This book is dedicated to my mom Kathleen Lee, Mark "Three Hawks" Steel, my family, friends and to you the reader. May you see the beauty that is all around you. Especially when it is not so easy.

JANUARY 1st

The Circle

The beautiful circle of life continues on as each day is not only a beginning, it is also an ending. A moment when you have crossed the veil to the other side of a moment and for a brief pause you are in that sacred space, the space that is in between. Be still long enough and you will not only find that peaceful space but you will feel the joy and excitement of knowing you are moving into a new and exciting space. A truly amazing part of your journey. When you stop to realize every moment has been an amazing moment, simply because it is! When things seem low, as they sometimes will, just remember that circle and know that you are coming around again to a simply beautiful part once again.

JANUARY 2nd

Possibilities Of A New Year

Intentions and hopes for a new and fresh start are often squashed by the hustle bustle of recapping the previous year. End of year reports, putting into a chart, a graph, a logical way to show your progress for the year gone by can often leave you feeling overwhelmed and discouraged about your fresh start. So, when you find yourself in this situation, take a moment to reflect on how amazing the past year was and remind yourself gently that all one can ever do is simply their best. Will there be room for improvement? Of course. But remember, you are exactly where you need to be now; otherwise you would be somewhere else. You accomplished what you were to do. So smile and take your next step into all the possibilities of a new year.

JANUARY 3rd

The Small Voice

That small voice and deep yearning that pops in your head to say, "Hey wouldn't it be cool to do this", or "go there" or "be like......"? The answer is always "Yeah that would be cool." But are you going to do those things? Are you really? Most of us think that we will clear up some things, be prepared, make some time. Only to realize you can't clear things up, you can't be prepared enough because for everything you check off of your list, two things get added, something gets shifted for something else that feels urgent. Usually things you feel like are being dictated by the world. So take this moment to realize that little small voice wants to be heard. It deserves for you to take enough time to listen. And just maybe you will finally be heard.

JANUARY 4th

A Different View

Keeping your head up and trusting that it will all be ok even if you can't see any type of solution is what we must all learn to do. God truly does work in the most amazing ways. Sometimes it's in the kindness of a friend, an unexpected blessing you never saw coming, or simply because you are you and somehow that is what matters. We tend to view ourselves, or our situation, with a different set of eyes, never taking a moment to adjust our vision, or to get a clearer look at the circumstances. But in a single moment God may send you a friend or an event that will allow you to see things differently; to see yourself differently. Ultimately that helps you see the world more clearly too!

JANUARY 5th

Change

Change. What a great word. Have you taken a moment to think about this word? What does it mean to you? How do you feel when you hear it? What does it take to create it? Well, the best friend to the word "change" is action. As long as you have these two together you're always getting things done. You can't have one without the other, because one creates the other and the other is required. What actions do you need to take to create change? And what changes are happening in your life that require action? Go deep inside yourself and introduce these two friends, because they are made for each other. Nurture and support their friendship within yourself and they will nurture and support you.

JANUARY 6th

Be Your Own Drummer

Sometimes in life you spend time feeling this yearning to do something, but you're not sure how. And often you don't even really know what it is you're wanting to do. Really all along you know exactly what it is, but you simply don't believe that you can or should be doing it. But you start to notice all the signposts that keep pointing to the same things. Oh my how your heart soars to imagine being and doing those things, being that person. And then you realize the only thing that is in your way is you. Sometimes we are our own worst problem. Funny how much easier it is to give credit to excuses. March to the beat of the world's drummer. We are not our circumstances. So take those classes, go to those seminars, take those trips and remember you really do create your own reality. Be your own drummer.

JANUARY 7th

Be The Light

Remembering your past can be as wonderful as you'd like it to be. You can also choose to dwell in regrets or blame and past hurts. Take a minute to really remember and then choose to look at your past from the bright side. A pitch black room cannot remain that way with just a single drop of light. Though the light might not be bright enough to illuminate the entire room, it is powerful enough to simply have its presence known. God says "Be the light you wish to see in the world." You have the choice to turn up your wattage, to shine as brightly as the sun. You also have the ability to simply be a nightlight. But in any case, remember that it's all up to you how you show up in this world.

JANUARY 8th

The Path To Spirit

The path we all travel toward Spirit is different for everyone. While we all end up in the same place - which is in Spirit itself, we each choose a different direction or avenue that takes us there. But what we know to be true is that we are not really going anywhere, because Spirit is right within each of us. The longest journey you will ever make is the path from your head to your heart. The lessons and experiences we have along the way are opportunities for us to grow in Spirit, to learn about who we really are. To remember that we are Spiritual beings having a human experience, not the other way around as some might think. Realizing that we are all connected to each other, yet responsible only for ourselves, is a valuable step as we live our lives and make our journey.

JANUARY 9th

Footprints Upon Our Heart

Stop to look around at the people who are in your life at this moment. We all have something to learn from each other. We also have something to teach. Many times in our lives we meet certain people who have such an impact on us that we are forever changed along the way. The friends and family we have help mold us along the way and, as we all have challenging relationships, sometimes it is then that we notice we are all mirrors to each other. We see things in others that we admire or despise, only to realize that those qualities are also present in us. But what a gift to know that we are all in this together and, though we will cross paths with many we can look back on our lives and see all the beautiful footprints that have been left upon our heart.

JANUARY 10th

Take Your Time

Daily life seems to travel at the speed of light. With our attention going in so many directions is it any wonder we spend our day feeling scattered and not really as present as we should be? We allow ourselves to get frustrated about things that don't really matter in the big scheme of it anyways. So remind yourself that what really does matter is you and finding your center something to focus on. Doing too many things, with a small amount of productivity, is what consumes most of the day. Take your time and really be present in the moments of your day. Time is a precious commodity, the thing we have the least of, and the very thing we really want the most. So in that still moment notice that you are the keeper of your clock you can't go any faster or slower, so relax and take your time.

JANUARY 11th

Reflect The Love Of Spirit

You hear shocking stories on the news about things you would never really imagine. And you wonder how someone could do that. What could possibly cause people to do such terrible things to each other? And then you notice that people are far worse to themselves. The way that one thinks can be as deadly to their body and soul as a bullet straight from a gun. Words can cut and wound worse than any knife. So take time to change your thoughts, your judgments and poisonous words to reflect the love of Spirit. For as much pain and hurt in the world that we see, it is also covered in tremendous love and courage. So open your eyes and look around you. And you will see the love that is longing to be heard and felt by all of God's children.

JANUARY 12th

Pieces Of The Puzzle

We have heard that everything happens for a reason. That nothing happens by chance. A higher order to things is always at work. We often lose track of this and walk around almost in a daze, not really realizing that every interaction is a small piece of the puzzle that is being put in place to make up the beautiful experience of our life. When we step back and look at things from an up above perspective, it is amazing to see how each experience and every person put in our path has been significant in painting the picture of our life. But as you are looking you can see that our painting is part of their painting and they all beautifully match into the much larger painting that includes us all. Spirit is the master artist.

JANUARY 13th

The Unattainable

What motivates a person? Some of us go through our day from one situation to the next without ever really stopping to see the goal we are trying to achieve. Some of us simply think we want something or someone in our lives for a variety of reasons, only later to discover it may have been more about the challenge of getting something that was always a little beyond our reach. As we set our sights on the thing or person that just keeps moving further away, we realize that we just seem to want it more. But is it really who or what we want? Or is it simply another attempt to fill a need within ourselves by proving we can attain the unattainable?

JANUARY 14th

Greener Grass

Sometimes we make decisions and choices in our lives that seem like the best or easiest idea at the time. On some level we know in our heart that maybe we should have done something different, but we still choose to do what we do. So why do we beat ourselves up when things don't go smoothly? Did we expect that they would? Well guess what, things went exactly as they should have. It may never make sense, and others may not agree or approve of our choices, but in the end the lessons will be learned and we will have had some very amazing experiences. Would things have been better if we would have chosen differently? Who knows? Many people think the grass is always greener on the other side of the fence. It's a great time to realize that all grass needs to be mowed.

JANUARY 15th

It Starts With You

Have you ever noticed how many people around you seem to need help?   While it is important to show kindness and compassion to others, it is far more important to be sure to honor yourself in the process. Many times we are so eager to help another that we completely lose ourselves along the way.   What we often fail to notice is that our help may indeed be a hindrance to the other person as well as to ourself.   By exerting all our time and energy to help fix another's problems we conveniently avoid working on our own.   We intend to get to those later.   But if we are not willing to love ourself enough to work on the one person we can change, what makes us think that our efforts will be successful on another?

JANUARY 16th

Trusting Another

The bonds and connections you make with others can be the biggest opportunity for us to learn about our self. When you meet another person who intrigues you, it is interesting to realize how exciting it can be to learn all about them. In sharing your story with them they find out about you but, more importantly, it helps you make peace with yourself. By opening your heart to share with another you are able to say to the world, "this is me and my experiences in life have helped mold me into the person I am". In trusting another you learn to trust yourself. When you have stopped judging yourself for your past, and learn to forgive and love yourself, it is amazingly easy to love others.

JANUARY 17th

The One

My life has been spent daily, every single day of it, with this one person. For as much time as I have spent with them I have just barely begun to know them. What has taken me so long to realize how amazing this person is? I spent many years criticizing this person, always making them feel less than good enough, and when someone else thought of them badly it only reinforced my feelings, too. I spent a lot of time looking for someone better to love; someone more deserving. Now that everyone else is gone, I am left alone once again with this person. What's different now is that I realize how much I love them and how much torment I put them through and they are still here loving me back. So each day I stand in front of this person, looking straight into their eyes and seeing the love coming back directly from the mirror I am looking into.

JANUARY 18th

Expectations

Expectations. So many people around us seem to have so many expectations of us. Take a minute to identify who has these expectations. Is it work, our spouse, our parents, our friends, our family, people we don't know? To some extent it is all of them. But really the biggest culprit of all is us. We have the most demanding expectations of ourselves. Are they even really fair? While some are justified and even healthy, if we take the time to stop and identify what these expectations are, and just who is responsible for them, we will then realize that, just as everything else, if we see how love may be involved then we will see our truth, and we will be aware of the real nature of the expectations and know that it all comes back around to us.

JANUARY 19th

Do Nothing

There are days when you should just be doing nothing. Once you decide to ignore that voice and the urge that says you should be doing this or doing that. The little myth that says if you aren't doing anything then nothing is getting done, that you're acting lazy. Have you ever stopped to realize just how unproductive it actually is to continue to push yourself without ever giving yourself a rest, a chance to unwind and shut all that noise up inside your head. Sometimes you just gotta get in your jammies and watch movies all day, decide not to drive your car anyplace. Even the car deserves a break. Decide to do nothing. Don't plot out your day and certainly don't set your alarm. Take some time to recharge, and you will realize that you actually got more done doing nothing than you ever thought possible.

JANUARY 20th

Perfect Timing

Can you think of a time when someone said the simplest thing to you, something you have always known anyway, and everything just seems to make sense at that exact moment? You respond as if this is the first time you've ever heard this, and certainly it's not something you'd give yourself credit for knowing. Why does it sound different and new? As you think about this new yet old piece of information, you process it through your mind to see how it fits and how it's not just a simple statement after all. It is indeed a truly profound thing and for a minute you wonder why you didn't really notice this before. What is Spirit teaching me in this moment? Then it occurs to you that maybe you weren't ready to receive even the simplest things until the right time. So remember all timing is perfect in the eyes of Spirit.

JANUARY 21st

Be Willing

One of the most challenging things is to sit with others and, as you become aware of how out of balance they seem to be, you deeply want to be able to share the knowledge you have received from finding your peaceful balance. Then you realize you can't share that with them if they aren't even aware that they are perpetuating the very madness they are trying to escape from. As they speak you hear them confirming those very actions that keep them in a state of fear and constant pain. And that's when you realize how grateful you are in that moment to have arrived in the place of the consciousness you are living in. Being willing to change and have an open heart are the greatest gifts you can give to yourself. Share these same gifts with those around you.

JANUARY 22nd

Milestone In The Journey

Often times we do not see our own progress. We encounter a great friend from our past and catch up on time gone by. That's when we are able to hear the recap of highlights of our previous days of time spent apart. The feedback and reactions we get show us just how much progress we have made. Day-to-day events that happen could very well be a milestone in your life. When something is happening we don't usually notice the significance at that moment. We need a little time and space to allow things to sink in and make sense. Honestly some things never make sense. But in any case every moment is a significant milestone in the journey of your life.

JANUARY 23rd

Details

So many people get stuck in the details, thinking so much about every little part of a drama. He said this, she did that, can you believe this and so on. Few people step back to look at the big picture. They can't see past all that drama, those justifications that make their choices ok. People get distracted and confused with those details. Getting distracted allows us to be all over the place. While it is important to focus and get a clear idea of just what is actually going on, it's more important to remember that, while details do have some relevance, it can become a huge tangled web. But even with a beautiful web, we must step back to see its true beauty.

JANUARY 24th

The Same Old Gift

Life gives us the most amazing learning opportunities. We do our work on ourself, and think we have mastered something so we move on to the next thing only to realize we may have more work to do on something we thought we had healed within ourself that seems all too familiar. And although it will have a different package it is the same old gift inside. Maybe this time we will look at the contents and see just what clues it can offer us about ourself. Maybe when we accept the lesson of that gift, it won't be presented so many times. Maybe we will value it and appreciate the opportunity to learn. Then we can graciously move on to the next part of our journey to self-discovery. Learning to accept all our gifts with love and appreciation will teach us to value the contents. We will realize then that contents in our gifts are what make up the contents of our heart.

JANUARY 25th

Turn Up The Wattage

It seems interesting that so many people simply walk around angry. They snap at anyone near them and act annoyed with how that person is being. Usually the other person isn't even doing anything. Observing complete strangers can often be the best opportunity to show yourself some compassion. It seems so silly to be annoyed about the smallest things. If we could all stop for a moment and take time to notice you can spend even less energy to be happy. And the results feel better. Then you notice happiness can be just as contagious as participating in drama. Try to be that mirror for those people by reminding them of the love that is right inside of them, it may be hard for them to see, but that's when you turn up the wattage. Blinding lights are hard to miss.

JANUARY 26th

Changing

There are so many things to do in this life, yet we spend our time doing the same old things we've always done, often times hoping for different results, a different life. Every person has their own mini-universe. They do things just a bit different from you and maybe they do things exactly opposite. The most amazing thing is that we have the freedom and the choice to do things anyway we dream. The secret is to wake up so that you can dream. People spend the day walking around and conducting their life and they keep wanting to live someone else's. Create the life you love living, be an example for others and they will be able to see an amazing new idea about how to change their life, too. Because we all know the only life we can change is our own.

JANUARY 27th

A Form Of Addiction

So many people have some form of addiction, whether it is alcohol, drugs or unhealthy relationships. As friends we want to be there to support whatever decision they try to make for themselves. It is often difficult for us to remain silently by as they self destruct.   And then we are reminded that we are all here to learn and love and what seems so unhealthy to someone may feel better to them than what they had before. How do you protect them from themselves? A better question would be how do you protect you from yourself?   Most of us are still trying to figure that one out.   But what I can say with certainty is that regardless of what you think the answer may be the only one that can help is Spirit.

JANUARY 28th

Move On

There comes a point in every situation when you have the realization that it may be time to move on from your current situations. People have a tendency to remain in that comfort zone for so long that it becomes hard to realize that you have become paralyzed to the circumstances; your comfort zone has become so uncomfortable that you can barely stand it. So why do you choose to stay? Most of the time it is simply because we are afraid that the unknown will bring us less than what we have in our life. We confuse predictability with security. We underestimate ourselves to the point that we resign to simply sitting in our own little world when all along we are trying to break out of our self made prison. Take a look and see that you are the only one standing between you and your freedom.

JANUARY 29th

Seeking Approval

Many times people yearn for the need to be wanted and valued. We walk around seeking the approval of others and hoping they will show us that we are wanted. The lengths that some people will go to, to fill this void, is absolutely amazing. Yet we have tremendous limitations set on ourself for taking risks that will enrich our lives. We feel discouraged when our great deeds go unnoticed and hurt when we don't get the recognition we deserve for our efforts. So take a minute to think about Spirit. We are valued and wanted in every second of every day of our entire existence. We are shown in so many ways how much we are appreciated for simply being who we are. So why is it that we still seek approval from everywhere and everyone when we have all we will ever need?

JANUARY 30th

In This Moment

When you are tuned into the frequency of your highest vibration you feel exhilarated. Everything seems to be going amazingly well. All the possibilities of new and exciting experiences seem to lift you right off the earth. It's almost like you are floating around on a cloud. It is in these moments that you are truly in touch with your childlike innocence because in those moments you are not attached to an outcome. You are just so enchanted with the moment. You are so happy to be in that moment that you are not thinking of the past and you are not the least bit concerned about the next one. All you know is that this moment feels amazing. You feel plugged straight in to the master source and then you realize this is how it feels to truly be connected to Spirit.

JANUARY 31st

Being Honest

Being honest is one of the most important qualities a person can have. We often feel like we are accomplishing so much in our efforts to be honest with others. So why is it often so difficult to be honest with ourself? I believe that we have such a fear of rejection, or even a sense of unworthiness, that we tell ourselves we want something different. So when things don't seem to work out the way we would like them to we are able to have a reason readily available. Sometimes in our disappointment we say so many things that we actually start to believe them and then we seem to not even notice that we are being insincere with ourself. Honesty begins within us, and although the truth can often be unpleasant for some to hear, I think we can all agree that honesty really is the best policy. Sooner rather than later.

FEBRUARY 1st

The Best Logic of All

How many times have you heard a voice in your head suggesting you follow thru with an idea, and you just know in your heart that you really want to but then your brain tries to throw in some logic or reasoning to work against it. Often we allow that to happen and we then make excuses and add more so called logic. What is the point to it? Maybe that voice is God speaking to you, hoping you will simply follow your heart and his suggestion. After all he knows your true heart. Hasn't your head had enough opportunities to make the decisions? Recently I had this exact experience, I heard the call, but I didn't feel like I had enough information or background and I was too concerned with what I thought someone else would think about me. To my surprise when I took the time to follow my heart, I discovered that being myself and following the voice is the best logic of all.

FEBRUARY 2nd

A New Day, Another Chance

Today was the day that I knew the name of this little inspirational book. Inspired by the connection with another I realized that no matter what you've done, or where you have been, or who you thought you were, when you wake up it is "A new day, another Chance". Take that chance, be who you were designed to be. Dig to the center of that vulnerable person who wants to come out. Give them a chance. Stop living in regret, for the lessons that you have lived. All is as it should have been. Often times when we are in the middle of a difficult situation, we get frustrated because we can't see clearly to the other side. We simply want to try and get through it and move on to the next thing, never taking the time to notice a part of our heart is shutting down. So open your eyes to the new day and another chance. Taking a chance is worth all the risk.

FEBRUARY 3rd

Take Care of Your Body

The body has a way of knowing that too much is going on. We are doing to much, not getting enough rest, but since we feel fine we keep on pushing ourselves. We throw ourselves out of alignment, not just physically but mentally as well. We keep telling ourselves if we don't get everything done we think we need to, then things will not be going well. As you know the body will tolerate just so much and then it will become unhappy with us. It is no longer at ease. That's when it happens. We get sick. Sometimes to the point that we can't even get out of bed. We have to slow down enough to take care of our body, to put our self back in harmony. So be mindful of your body and make sure that you give it what it needs. All those things that you need to do will be waiting for you and your healthy body to do them.

FEBRUARY 4th

A Perfect Love

We all have an idea of how a perfect love with another should be. We see romantic movies and we yearn for that magical love that we see develop on the screen. As we watch from an outside perspective it is easy to see two strangers destined to meet walking one street apart toward each other. We sit on the edge of our seats yelling to them to turn now, your true love is right there. But they don't hear us, and why would it be so obvious if they simply did turn then to see before them the perfect love. From an outside perspective we can see all the qualities that these two have that match the other perfectly. We know what has been going on to lead them to where they are now, but neither of them do. We all know the qualities we would love in another. Honesty, integrity, strength, courage, loving, kind, gentle- to name a few. But as we grow we realize it takes time to see these qualities. It takes time to learn from another. Most importantly we must develop these qualities in our self to be able to recognize them in another.

FEBRUARY 5th

Spontaneity of Spirit

Sometimes in life we encounter circumstances that we can't really make sense of. Maybe we meet someone that we are totally drawn to but we are not really sure on what level. It is nice to have time and space with that person to walk through the experience and not have all the answers to what is going on. While being clear about ones feelings, will give you a place of reference, it is also a blessing to leave things open and unlimited. Sometimes the boundaries we place on situations based on our lack of knowledge about the circumstances takes away the very magic of having the opportunity to experience the spontaneity of Spirit. If we remain open to all possibilities we will be amazed to see outcomes beyond what we would have imagined for ourselves.

FEBRUARY 6th

The Balance Of A Vulnerable Heart

Being vulnerable can be quite uncomfortable at times. Often we will close up our heart to avoid feeling this way. It can be challenging to find the balance between the two. The fear of being hurt or ridiculed often is so strong that we are unwilling to even allow ourselves to open up to others. We notice that others have the same fear. When we realize our own strength it gives us courage to take a chance and know that when we keep our heart open and allow ourselves the opportunity to be vulnerable with others, it sets a great example for them and relationships can move to a whole new level. So remember that whatever happens, you have enough love in your heart to have an amazing experience. If you get hurt, your heart will surely heal as it has been practicing.

FEBRUARY 7th

Get Clear

Have you ever tried to look through a really smeared window? It is possible, but our view is surely not so clear. Often time's people operate in this hazy cloud. They don't really know what is going on around them and they certainly don't know what is going on in them. We get frustrated when what we ask for is misunderstood. If we simply stop and take a moment to clear things up, we would see that if only we would seek some clarity on the situation it would help us communicate with others and it would give us a good idea about what we need from others. Getting clear will help us realize what we need from ourselves as well as help us communicate with others about what we are asking of them. Stop wasting time looking through clouded eyes, and you will finally see the truth.

FEBRUARY 8th

Worth The Hurt

Sometimes in life we have experiences that seem to leave us wondering was it worth the hurt we are feeling. Then we realize that if we weren't feeling hurt then it would have been because we had not felt love. Feeling love is what it's all about. So we wonder was it worth it? YES it's always worth it. Why do we seem to hesitate about taking a step forward into an experience? On our journey we have been reminded many times that we always make it through to another moment. The experience is just a flash, a small burst of light that helps illuminate the path we are traveling. Every experience has a lesson in it for us to learn, to learn who we really are. To realize we are all connected and to remind us the importance of what it means to feel, to hurt and to learn to love once again.

FEBRUARY 9th

The Perfect Amount Of Time

People come into our lives and stay with us for a while. Others move on. We have many opportunities to experience so many wonderful relationships. Many times we choose to stay longer than we should and other times we long for more time. We blur the lines of completion and keep searching for a closure that is never really needed. When we take the time to look at those we have known, it is very clear that people are in our life forever. Whether it is simply a memory, a thought, a wish or a vision, we know they were with us for the perfect amount of time. They were with us for the time we needed them. The relationship was served, the experience was had and the time came to move on to yet another chapter in the book of our life. Each character played a unique part in our story, just as we have played the part for others.

FEBRUARY 10th

What Will You Do?

Sometimes we are faced with circumstances that force us to grow. Things come up in a relationship that challenges us in a way that may require an action or uncomfortable confrontation or conversation. While we struggle with how or what we should say that would make a difference, we know what we would do in the situation and we defiantly have an opinion of what we think the other person should do as well. And then we realize that no matter what we say, how much support we try to show, they are going to do what they are going to and that is really the bottom line. So what is it that we are going to choose to do? While we may or may not agree with the decision they make, we do have an obligation to make our own choice. What s best for us in the situation? Honor that and you will realize what matters most is your own balance and well-being.

FEBRUARY 11th

Everyday Miracles

When we make a conscious choice in our life to focus on what is important to us, we will be amazed at how many things we do every day that actually side track us from our own happiness. We have spent so much time worrying about all the things that we don't really care about, and the things we do care about simply pass us by. In all the hustle bustle we often don't even notice all the opportunities that appear every day. So imagine how even less obvious it was to us that we missed one of our miracle moments. How foolish are we to think that we don't have a fair chance when we our self tip the odds against our own favor. So when we finally open our eyes to all that is around us and witness all the unfolding miracles, it seems so silly that we hadn't noticed before. The best part is, we keep getting more opportunities once we have the eyes to see them.

FEBRUARY 12th

Burst Out Of Your Box

Often times when we feel stretched to our limits and are really not sure of the solution to anything going on, that's when it is time to slow down and remember that somehow everything always works out. The limitations we put on our self often leave us feeling squished into the box we have been living inside of. Stretch your arms out wide to accept all the amazing things Spirit has to offer and you will see the lid simply burst off the box. We all just need a little room to see past all the obstacles that seem to appear in attempts to keep us from allowing our self to succeed. It seems silly we complain about the box we are in when outward appearances may show us that it is us that is holding on so tightly to the lid. All the while we are screaming to have it removed. Just let go.

FEBRUARY 13th

Learning To Know

We meet new people and we feel inspired to know all about them. What do they like, where do they live, and who are they? As we take the time to learn about them we often realize the intensity of the quest for knowledge changes. It either intensifies or weakens based on our interactions with them. The same can be said for our search of knowledge with in our self. The time we take for our self and the interactions we have will determine the intensity of the knowledge we learn about our self. Most times we sit and judge things, either about the other person or our self. Once we get past the judgments and labels we find that is when the real learning begins.

FEBRUARY 14th

Say What You Need To Say

Why is it that so many people can't just say what needs to be said? They worry about how the other person will react to what they have to say. So rather than just say it they will try to word it in such a way that will make it easier for the other person to hear. Often what needs to be said is altered in such a way that it comes out and sounds nothing like what it should. We don't want them to be mad at us for speaking our truth. What a disservice we do to each other, for although the truth is sometimes hard to hear, if our own loved ones can't be honest with us, then who will? Difficult conversations are very scary, but what is scarier is when everyone avoids what needs to be said. Strangely enough we always end up in the same place, so have that conversation sooner rather than later and get on with the love minus the drama. In the process we will learn to be honest with our self.

FEBRUARY 15th

Open To Receive

Open to receive. How is it that we expect things to happen in our life when many times we are closed down? We try to do things for others, but when it comes time for someone to do something for us we have a hard time accepting it. Whether it's a kind deed, a genuine compliment or simply meeting a need we might have, we feel gratitude, but it is followed by something else. Perhaps you are not open to receive. Receiving is as important as giving. Without both there is no balance. What is it that Spirit is teaching you about yourself that is causing you to feel unworthy of such gifts? It all comes down to forgiveness. Be gentle with yourself and know that by not graciously receiving from others you are limiting their joy and quite possibly keeping them from the beauty in the lesson that we all learn.

FEBRUARY 16th

Where Is Your Attention?

It has been said that what you put your attention to is what you bring about. Have you taken a moment to think about what you are giving your attention to? While most situations or circumstances require some action and attention on our part, it is often obvious after the fact that we spent more than enough of our valuable attention on something that was probably handled in a very short time. How many things did we miss out on simply because our attention was doing double time where it was no longer needed? Learning to balance our time and attention often takes a life time to master, but one thing you can count on is a number of opportunities to practice the art of learning this balance. Expand yourself and take charge of how you spend your valuable resources and you will find a huge return on your investment.

FEBRUARY 17th

Love What Your Doing

We work hard to accomplish goals and dreams we have. Sometimes we get so caught up in the outcome and how to navigate around all the obstacles placed in our way, that we lose track of the love and fun that should be present in our actions. We allow our self to get stressed out about how we perform at our tasks, what others will think, and if we are really good enough to deserve what we are working towards. We often realize that we are not performing at our best because we are bogged down with worry. So take a minute to remember why you are doing what you're doing. Go out there and have fun. Allow yourself to feel the love of what you're doing, and you will realize that everyone will see that amazing energy and suddenly things really aren't hard after all.

FEBRUARY 18th

A Surge Of Confidence

Why is it that when someone else has a strong belief in us and our abilities we seem to feel a surge of new found confidence and energy? Often it is that surge that pushes us to the next level, that level that is just a little more than we've been doing. As their excitement and encouragement of us grows our confidence seems to bloom as well. As you go through your day and interact with others be mindful of the encouragement you may be able to give to them. You might be the one person that helps them move to the next level. You will come to realize that we are all open vessels through which Spirit flows. We are in fact hearing the voice of God through those people that believe in us. We are also speaking the voice of God. So take a minute to believe in yourself as God believes in you.

FEBRUARY 19th

Accept Things For What They Are

We try to give people the benefit of the doubt by thinking they will show us the respect that we show them. So why do we get disappointed with them when they continue the pattern? We too continue to give them yet another opportunity. At what point do we finally decide to stand our ground and see the circumstances for what they are? Apparently they are showing you how they truly feel. So why do we make excuses or try to rationalize all the reasons they are acting as they are. Sometimes it can be as simple as accepting things for what they are; deciding on how you will choose to react or what part you will play. People can only treat you as you allow them too. Once you have had enough you simply choose again and move on. Set the example of the respect you want shown by others by living from it for yourself.

FEBRUARY 20th

Out Of Sight Out Of Mind?

The saying "Out of sight out of mind" has been said so often, but have you really ever stopped to analyze just what it means? When we see things and they are right in front of our eyes we feel like we have no choice but to acknowledge them. Isn't it a bit unusual that when we aren't faced with something we have several tactics we will use to avoid it, and pretend like we don't really need to deal with it unless it is staring us in the face. So what do you think makes the exact situation either more or less urgent based on whether or not it is in our view or not? Either way we know those things are there waiting for our attention. On some level we always realize that our physical sight is only just one reminder to us to let us know that we have the ability to see with far more than our eyes. Use your heart and mind and you will see the solution.

FEBRUARY 21st

Never Assume

One of the four agreements written about by Don Miguel Ruiz is to never assume anything. We don't always have all the information at times and in those situations that go other than how we wish they might, we start to assume things about why this or that may have happened. Often times we are angry or hurt and think that someone intentionally set out to make our life more difficult or that they don't care about us because maybe they said they'd call and didn't. And while we sit around waiting, we allow our mind to wander. That's when those old tapes start playing and we convince our self we know all the details, when all along we simply know only our version. So take the time to remember that we must give others the opportunity to be who they are and let them do what they do or don't do, all the while we remain true to who we are and what we do.

FEBRUARY 22nd

Sharing Time With Others

Spending time with others is a simple way to demonstrate that we care about them. You don't always have to have something to say or something to do. It is simply just sharing your space and energy. That unspoken knowing that your there is really what most people long for. Whether it is a child, a spouse, a friend or relative we all want to feel that connection. That peaceful feeling that has no words yet knows all feelings. When you tear down all those walls and conditions and you set your heart free to do what it was created to do, you will realize the impact of unconditional love. Just as there is nothing a child could do that would cause their parent not to love them, there is also nothing we could do to lose the love of Spirit. That sharing of time is the purest form of love available to us all and through us all.

FEBRUARY 23rd

Do You Really Want This?

There are things in life we want. We really want it. We've dreamed of it for years. And then that day comes where what you want is right in front of you and its real. You make the decision that you are going to do what it takes to finally have one of your dreams. And that's when it happens, you walk confidently into the situation, but a hesitation comes. You start to think of all the reasons that maybe you should wait, even though everything is lining up perfectly and it makes more sense to you why you should have what you want. But you make an attempt to convince yourself that you don't deserve to have it, you feel selfish. It's not so simple you say and then you're asked, "Do you really want this? Yes or No? Yes you answer. Well then it really is that simple. Take a chance and live, you have been waiting long enough.

FEBRUARY 24th

Peaceful Knowing

We make a decision to walk the path with Spirit, our path, not someone else's. We take responsibility for our actions, our lives, and who we are becoming. We participate in a life that is spiritually nurturing. It feels so amazing, you have a confidence that shines like the sun. You're aware of the things that you'd really love to have in your life but for the first time you're willing to slow down and be patient with a peaceful knowing that the life you've dreamed of is on the way. It is close enough you can feel it. You still don't know how it will happen but you realize when you walk with Spirit you have that peaceful understanding that it will all manifest into reality, whether you understand it or not. All it takes is an open heart and the willingness to simply say yes. Spirit will work out the details.

FEBRUARY 25th

Disappointment

Sometimes in life we experience things that don't go as we wish they would. We feel let down at the situation and we often feel frustration with our self for getting our hopes up about something we were looking forward too. It can be challenging to take a step back and see the blessing in disguise that is cloaked in the clothing of disappointment. But we should see the positive side that is available to teach us the lesson that is coming through. Rather than feel a sense of finality of the loss of a temporary setback, look at what might be a reason it isn't working out for right now and know that in the big scheme of things it really will make sense. So instead of closing down with another disappointment be proud of yourself for making the attempt to go after something you want and be thankful that you've chosen to step up and keep trying. It will work out in the perfect time and in the perfect way.

FEBRUARY 26th

Opportunity To Express

Sometimes you are so aware of Spirit in your life that you feel an almost electric feeling. People and events often make us feel this same way. It is like being in love, your stomach is nervous and you are full of energy. Your heart is actually expanding in you and you wonder if maybe you will burst. The challenge can be how does one remain in this state more often than in the "less than" state we often reside in? Once you realize that people or events that make you feel this way are actually put in your path so that Spirit can show you love through your experiences. You have the opportunity to express what you are feeling back to the world around you. The way you perceive is the key to the way you receive. So keep your heart open and enjoy the journey.

FEBRUARY 27th

You Are The Common Denominator

We often walk around just doing what we do never noticing the affect we have on those around us. What example are you setting? How are you choosing to show up in this world? Many times we focus on the things we may have done to hurt others or perhaps what they have done to hurt us. But at what point do you take some ownership of the very choices you have made that have brought into your life the very circumstances that you may or may not enjoy? While we are correct to notice that things that we have been through have set the course for whom we have been becoming. Don't be deceived by the notion that everything and everyone has caused all your problems. When you look at the common denominator in all your problems you will realize the only consistent thing has been you and your interpretation of your life. Instead of trying to fix all that's around you, start with the one who has been there, you.

FEBRUARY 28th

Showing That You Care

What really matters are the genuine moments that show you care and are thinking of another. We often think people should just know how we feel. After all they know us don't they? But do we really even know our self? Whether we know how someone feels or not, it feels so wonderful to hear them say those things we think we know. That confirmation adds a spark to our day. Just taking a minute to say, "hey I was thinking about you and wanted to say hi" is such a simple thing to do but it makes a difference. If we really did take the opportunity to truly set the example of how we want to be treated by simply extending that to others, we'd send a clear message to those we love and those that we meet throughout our journey. We would come to understand that we have the ability to make peace on earth by first starting in our life.

FEBRUARY 29th

Every Day Is A Leap Year Day

Leap year gives us an extra day every four years. How and why is a mystery. Most of us have not really taken much time to get the details on this occurrence. We just simply know it is that way and we are ok with it. So when leap year rolls around we get a reminder that we have been given an extra day. We value it and notice that it only comes along ever so often. But what about the new day we are given every day? The one that is not guaranteed in any way but we wake up to another chance to live a brand new day. Walking in Spirit reminds us that really every day is truly a leap year day. The comfort in knowing we don't have to wait four years to receive an extra day is truly an amazing mystery and gift that we take for granted. So live your leap every day and value every moment.

MARCH 1st

Enjoy The Rain

Trying to plan out every detail of your life is like trying to count raindrops. You will waste valuable time trying to accomplish something that in the big scheme of things really won't add the security you are trying to achieve. Why set goals and boundaries that will limit you to the details when you can lift your eyes to Spirit and simply enjoy the rain. Many of the biggest blessings in our life happen to be the very things we don't plan. The unexpected miracles that show up and make life exciting. We tend to over think things and often we talk ourselves out of doing the very things that we truly love because it may not fit into our plans. So take a minute to look back on all the plans you have made in your life, now look back at the plans made by Spirit. It's easy to see that the unexpected miracles in your life are the plans that matter most.

MARCH 2nd

Set Sail

Many times we have in mind how we would like something to go. We have this deep feeling of knowing that really can't be explained, much less make any sense. So why is it that we tend to let our minds wander into the thoughts and ideas that have absolutely no business even being a thought? Our fear of rejection and disappointment keep us living in this crazy state of wonder. While wonder in another respect can be a healthy idea, it can also be a destructive thing when paired up with a negative notion. So when we set our sails to a destination and feel the wind coming to help, as long as we are pointed in the correct direction we will notice that our path may not be exactly as we thought it should go, but we will discover that we will arrive at our desired point in life as soon as we decide to set sail. Remember the beauty in the journey is what makes our destination so valuable.

MARCH 3rd

Who Are You Choosing To Be?

When one is faced with a set of choices it is important to stop and evaluate who you are living as while you make a decision. While all the options you have may be something you desire on some level, it's important to pause long enough to try and see the bigger picture. We all know that every choice and decision has a set of actions and consequences that will go hand in hand with it. While sometimes our choices won't hurt another or in fact have nothing to do with another, it does have an effect on us. So while a decision may contain a short term outcome or be a stepping stone to something more lasting it is truly your choice to decide based on what is in your own highest good. So look at what and who you are choosing to be in your decisions and you will find that is what builds your character.

MARCH 4th

All Things Will Fall Into Place

It is an amazing experience when we have that moment of clarity and can see just how Spirit works in our life when we finally allow ourselves to be open and willing to learn. By our own patience and willingness to truly believe that our highest good is always being met, it makes it so simple to be ok with choices or decisions that we have made that may have turned out differently than we hoped at the time. We have the opportunity to be the observer of our own life and in that moment we can truly be grateful for things going in a different way. What we think we may want in our life may just be another opportunity for us to settle. Often when we do this we find that it is not really what we wanted after all. God always has the best in store for us if we truly trust that all things fall into place.

March 5th

Seek New Questions

Often times we long for the peace of security. We want to know all the answers to the never ending questions that seem to pop up in our daily life. What are the questions that are popping up in your life? What are you giving your attention to? To feel at peace within yourself you must start with the realization that unanswered questions are the very things that encourage us to move past where we are. We move forward seeking answers. It might be time to move forward with new questions, as you seek these questions, the ones that bring great meaning to your life, you will then realize that the answers are actually contained within our searching. When we stop searching for the answers, it is then that they will find us.

MARCH 6th

Take A Chance On Yourself

There is a time in one's life when it is important to slow down and make a conscious decision to find out about yourself. We spend much effort and energy when we have an interest in another. Why is it that we are unwilling to extend this courtesy to a stranger yet when it comes to our self we don't make any effort at all. We carefully consider this other persons feelings and we make every effort to make them feel comfortable in a hope that they will trust us, like us or even fall in love. Look at how we treat our self. Are we not important enough to get to know? How can we expect someone else to be willing to take a chance on us when we are unwilling to do it for our self? If someone else treated us the way we often treat ourselves would we really be a true friend?

MARCH 7th

Don't Lose Track Of The Bigger Picture

Being willing to stand for what you believe in can be very different from defending your need to be right. We often lose track of the bigger picture. We get caught up in the details and our expected outcome. While all the while we may be hurting the person we are in conflict with. What do we stand to gain by tearing someone down so that we may stand proudly on top of their defeat? When you are willing to speak your truth to someone, it is simply that, it is it is not an attempt to change their view and bring them around to your way of thinking. Simply say what you need to and then listen to them. Show the respect that you would like to be shown and rise above to see the bigger picture. It is then you will notice there is enough room for everyone.

MARCH 8th

True Giving

Doing something nice for others can be very rewarding. It can also bring unnecessary disappointment if you have attached how you think they should react. If you have done something in hopes of recognition or to impress someone, you then need to reevaluate what is motivating your actions. While everyone wants to be appreciated and valued it is simply in the giving that will bring a true appreciation. So someone doesn't show you the reaction you may have wanted, but it is in your own interpretation of the situation that will devalue the true gift. Not all people show how they feel in the same way. It doesn't mean that they are any less thankful for the gift you have given. Don't rob yourself of the true gift. It doesn't depend on how it is received, it simply is in the way you give it that matters.

MARCH 9th

You Are The Lead Role In Your Story

When we step into the lead role of our own life, it is then that we can start to enjoy all the different parts and story lines that we will play. Too often we choose to always be the supporting role in someone else's story. We live our life based on how we fit into theirs. While we play many parts and roles throughout our story, it gets very boring to everyone if we keep on choosing the same old roles, the same old story lines and the part of nothing more than an unpaid extra. How many scenes will it take for us to finally realize that we are more than qualified for any part we choose to play? Are we so silly to think that someone else is more qualified to be the lead role in our own story?

M ARCH 10th

Ever Changing

Time moves by so quickly, one day you are starting a new adventure and before you know it, it is a completely new experience. Often times we get so caught up in our lives that we don't notice all the changes going on right before our eyes. We see a person who hasn't been around in a while and it takes them only a glance to see how much things have changed. We lose track of time and space and what seems to be yesterday or last year was really 18 years ago. The journey of our life is ever moving forward and while we often get stuck in some of our circumstances it is clear that we are still evolving all the while. Look at your life from a higher perspective and you will see just how much you have really grown.

MARCH 11th

Take Time To Enjoy

There are people and situations that come into our life that help us realize who we are and who we are not. And while we may have had a strong connection to what we may have had, or what we were working towards there comes a moment when you must simply honor things for what they are and make a step forward. While your heart may ache or you may want to cry for what is no longer, it is important to be grateful for these lessons and gently remind yourself that the purpose was served and we must advance on to our next experience. Maintaining our center in a world of chaos can be challenging, but these are the lessons that help define us. Take the time to enjoy your life, your situations, your lessons, while they are happening, because as you've learned time is just a blip and is ever changing.

M ARCH 12th

Just Show Up

One has much to learn by the circumstances they are a part of. We often think we know how an outcome may be prior to even beginning a situation. So a lot of time is wasted in worry or concern for what may or may not occur, then when we we have finally played out every possible scenario we finally surrender to the realization that whatever is going to happen will, and in the way it should. So when you are about to walk into an unusually challenging situation breath in and remember to ask yourself "what can I learn from this experience? You may be surprised to find that when you just show up and get present in the moment everything will fall into place and will make perfect sense. It's not our job to try so hard, we are human beings, so our job is to be.

MARCH 13th

Maybe It's Time To Move On

It can often be difficult to stay balanced when you are faced with difficult people or situations. When these things come up it is usually an opportunity for us to grow in some way. And while we may feel angry or frustrated with what is going on, it just might be the uncomfortable situation that you need to push you out of that comfort zone you've been sitting in. Maybe things are just that frustrating so that you are unable to make excuses of why you should stay in that situation, or maybe you won't be able to justify all the reasons you feel obligated to make things work. Sometimes things just don't work anymore and it is time to move on to the next thing in your life. Just maybe that's why things are going as they are.

March 14th

Remove Your Own Bricks

The things that other people do, often have little or nothing to do with us. Yet we get stuck in the idea that somehow it does. We think that because they are not calling or making an attempt to contact us, that they probably aren't thinking about us either. But think about that for a moment. Do you call or contact someone every time you think about them? Probably not, but you still know that they matter to you. You continue to pray and hold that space in your heart and often your thoughts. Often times the things others do or say is really a reflection of how they are feeling within themselves. They act out in anger or demand something from us as an attempt to maintain some measure of control or as away to protect themselves by building a wall. Remember the bricks in the walls we have built, must be removed one by one and by our self.

MARCH 15th

Care For Yourself

Taking care of yourself is the first step to living the life you love. When you are tired and frustrated your body will start to slow down and things will seem to get harder. What does taking care of yourself mean? If a sick child came to you seeking help what would you do? First you would try to identify what is wrong. What is causing them to feel bad?   What can I do to fix this so you will feel better? It could be a simple fix, such as simply taking a nap, it could require a few adjustments and patience for the solution to start working, but it could be more than you can fix and you'd need to seek out more qualified help. But the bottom line is the same; we really want to help others. Just remember it starts with us. We can't help others until we've learned to care for ourselves first.

M ARCH 16th

Metaphysical- Beyond What You Know

Metaphysical- what a great word. Beyond the physical. More than what we see. Everything in life has a metaphysical meaning, every story, every situation, every person. Look at the storylines of your life, see them as they are, but then look a little further so you can see the meaning that extends beyond the physical. We are more than our physical self. We are not our circumstances. All things that happen have many levels of meaning. Life gives us many opportunities to grow and learn, as well as teach others. Our life's journey is all about self discovery, finding out who we are and why we are here. So although we have come here and have been given a physical body to learn in, we have been given so much more. Go beyond what you know.

MARCH 17th

Release

As we go through the experiences of our life, it is often necessary to release things. We know that these things no longer serve us, so why do we feel so anxious about this process? Are we worried about what feelings and emotions may come up during this release? We often get caught up in the "what if's" and the could have beens, and our minds drift to the great parts of that experience and that's when we realize why it is so important to follow thru with the release. We tend to stay in situations hoping things will be different all the while we failed to notice that they are different, but still as they should be. So follow that voice and know that we must release in order to move forward.

M ARCH 18th

Believing

It has been said that whether you think you can or can't do something, your right. Remind yourself that you can and if you choose not to do something it was because of a choice you made, not because you were unable. Believing is the most important step to accomplishing your goals, your desires and your dreams. Believing in yourself, the universe and the fact that Spirit wants you to be happy and successful is your first step, whether it's a baby step or a leap, either way you will get there. Be consistent and patient and most of all take action. Put one foot in front of the other as you walk your path straight into all your dreams. Spirit will show you the way. Remember no one ever got anywhere by standing in the same spot.

MARCH 19th

What Part Are You Choosing To Play?

People and circumstances come into our life to help us grow into the next stage of learning. What part are we playing in that process? Often people choose the role of the victim, that life is happening to them. Don't get caught up in this limiting thinking because life happens through you. Make a new choice, get a different view, or take a minute to really look at the situation to see what lessons are at work for you to learn. Accept them gently and realize that things can be as difficult or as painless as we make it. What can you learn about yourself when these situations arise? Maybe you will see that Spirit is at work and walking right beside you as you travel through yet another step on your journey.

MARCH 20th

Plugged In To Spirit

There are those days where everything is so amazingly perfect. The weather is great, you're with people you love and you're doing things that feel peaceful and fun. You realize in those moments that what is really many hours feels like it was only two hours. Even the things that would bother you on a day like this, they simply don't matter. As you enjoy every moment you realize that you are in no hurry to enter the next moment. When we are in the flow of our highest vibration time seems to no longer exist. The feeling we get in a space like this must be the way it feels to be plugged in directly to Spirit, for in these moments we truly appreciate all the gifts this life has to offer and what is yet to come.

MARCH 21st

A True Friend

Being a true friend often means that you must be patient and respect that others may choose differently than you do. And that is ok because they have their own set of lessons to learn. We often travel our path awhile with others, but ultimately we all travel our own path. When we realize what it means to be a true friend it is then that we will have the peace and comfort to know that everything always works out as it should. While we often feel the pain of our friends, as well as our own, it is important to remember that pain also serves a great purpose. For all experiences have a beautiful duality. Often we are carried forward in the simple knowing that Spirit is the one that brings us our true friends and shows us how to be one.

M ARCH 22nd

Motivation For Change

Often times we will become frustrated with someone or something. When this happens it is important to notice how you behave or react to what is going on. Many times we feel the need to prove we are right or are justified in our actions. We become upset when we are challenged about every action we make, or when we feel like the things we do go unappreciated or noticed. Giving up the need to be right and watching how the experience plays out will often times provide us with the satisfaction of knowing that everything will work out as it should in the proper time. The frustration you may feel in that moment may be Spirit pushing you to expand beyond your current situation. Discomfort is often the motivation for change.

MARCH 23rd

What We Wish For

The statement be careful what you wish for, has such a tremendous meaning. We don't always think about what things would be like once we got the things we wished for. Many times we wish for something that is so much less than what Spirit has in store for us. The very thing we wish for may be a hurtful lesson in the disguise of a new relationship or situation that may truly turn out to be a burden to us in the long run. Just remember that you will always be able to reach your dreams and all your wishes will come true. So the ones that don't work out in the ways you had hoped are simply your bigger self working things out for you on the levels you can't quite see yet. So keep looking forward to what is in store for you and know you deserve it.

MARCH 24th

Just Be

When you sit and watch nature you can see how peaceful and effortless it is to just BE. Birds fly and sing and are amazingly beautiful, they are not worried about bills or where they will sleep and if the other birds approve of them or even like them. They simply do what they do. The fact that they are able to fly and be free is also simply quite amazing. But it is no more amazing then the way Spirit created us. The big difference is we have the choice to not be what we could be. We choose to get caught up in the trivial things that don't matter. We forget that everything we will ever need is right inside of us. We too have the freedom to fly, open your heart, spread your arms wide to accept the life you were created to live and then you shall learn how to fly.

MARCH 25th

Disappointing Yourself

Some situations put us in a difficult position. We are called to make choices that may leave someone disappointed. Once we realize that, if we learn to honor our self and be clear with others about what we need and what we are unwilling to tolerate then we notice that the choices are not quite as hard as we made them out to be. What makes things hard is our desire to try and please everyone while barley squeezing our self into the situation. Many times our feeling of trying to make everyone else happy leaves us completely drained, unhappy and often resentful of the fact that we are cheating our self of our own peace. We feel stuck and many times we blame everyone and everything around us for how difficult things have become. Take a step back and choose again. Choose for you. Stand for you and realize that the person who has disappointed you was yourself.

M ARCH 26th

Trust And Respect Yourself

By trusting others to realize they know what is right for them, we also learn to trust our self. By giving respect to those around us we can see that all people really desire the same things from each other. While some people search for acceptance from others, they fail to notice that if only they would give unconditional acceptance to the people in their lives they too would feel that sense of acceptance that they have been longing for. Without trust and a genuine respect for others it will be impossible for us to get the very things we desire from another, for just as we fail to extend those qualities to them, we fail to honor those qualities within our self. Do we trust and respect our self? For we are the person to start with and once we have accomplished this, it is easy to learn to share this with others.

MARCH 27th

Participate In The Lesson

When we look back on our past year it is easy to see where we have been. When you're just starting an experience it is difficult to see where it is you might end up. Many times if we knew the lessons that are coming up we would be quite reluctant to even participate. But participation is exactly what we must do, for our lesson has come and with it comes great blessings. And while we may not see the circumstances as a blessing we will come to understand in time, why things had to unfold as they did. And while we may not see where it is that we will end up, we can rest assured that we will be protected along the way and while we may be unable to see the bigger picture from our view, trust in the fact that Spirit can see quite clearly for us if we will just trust.

MARCH 28th

Create A New You, Create A New Life

Why is it that some people are so full of anger and hate towards others? Often they have been hurt but instead of seeing the lesson that is at work they blame everyone and everything around them for what has gone wrong in their life. Oh my childhood was bad, my marriage failed because my spouse did me wrong. No one understands me. If only I was doing this I would finally be happy, if my boss would be more understanding, if my children would behave and the list goes on and on. So these people filled with anger at the world struggle to manipulate the situations around them hoping to finally get control of life. The lesson in finding peace and happiness is to look within and realize that we are creating our life. So if your unhappy create a new you and you will create a new life.

MARCH 29th

Inexperience

Often times others people's inexperience in a situation may leave us feeling over extended and frustrated. It is easy to observe the fact that they may need to observe what is going on around them and establish proper boundaries and develop a respectful relationship to those that have more experience in this area. So why is it so hard for us to do the same thing when we encounter this type of person? Is it a lack of knowledge of the other party that leaves us feeling the need to explain and justify things, or is it a feeling of distrust in their motives? While one may never know, it is important to focus on what it is that we do know. All will happen as it should. If we remain true to our own integrity and values we will be able to maintain our own healthy boundaries, while learning yet another lesson.

MARCH 30th

Precious Moments

It is easy to get swept up in a situation that makes you feel exhilarated. The ups and downs of our daily life sometimes leave us longing for the next moment we will feel this way. We must be careful of this cycle because while we are counting down the moments that will lead us to the next one we are looking forward to, we are missing the one that is happening. We put so much thought into the possible experience that we fail to add any pizzazz to our current moment. Instead of disregarding moments that may very well be our last, we should put effort into creating every moment as if it is all we will have. And while it is healthy to look forward to moments in which we know will be exciting, it is also healthy to live to our fullest potential in every moment for they are all truly precious.

MARCH 31st

The Stories Of Humans

We all have something to say, a story to share. But who is it really that we are sharing it with? Why do we feel the need to share it at all? It is quite simple, while we think we may be telling our own story, it in fact is also the story of our people. The human beings that we have come to be are all very much connected. And while the details may be different the overall story is the same. We have all chosen to come here in an experience called life that will challenge us to remember the things we have always known and provide us with opportunities to serve Spirit. Learning to love is what it all comes down to. Not only do we struggle to learn how to love others we often times have no concept of loving our self. The stories we tell and the stories we hear are all insights on how to master our divine right and that is to be the love we are searching for.

A PRIL 1st

Take Things In A Light Hearted Way

April fools day seems a bit odd because it is the one true day that you expect everyone to be joking, pulling pranks, and being quite dishonest at our expense to get a laugh or make a fool out of us. At least on this day you are expected to fess up, laugh together at the seemingly innocent act of purposefully being dishonest. Amazingly enough it is a day like any other day or holiday that is observed. Such serious things we take in a light hearted way because we are expected to. A great lesson can be taken from this foolish day of celebration and that is to light heartedly accept situations in which you are feeling foolish. Know that it will soon pass and a growing opportunity will be presented. So whether you're deceived on purpose or simply taken advantage of bring your light heart to the situation and your heart will definitely add to the light.

APRIL 2nd

Turn You Life Over

Finding time to quietly reflect gives the mind an opportunity to rest, a chance to refocus and quiet the chaotic noise that often takes over. A lot of time is spent avoiding those things which hurt us and others around us. We stay busy in an attempt to fool ourselves into thinking everything is okay when in fact on some level we are barely holding together. If you notice all the things in which you fell short of a goal or had some disappointment in life you will see that you where trying to run your own life, and while it is our responsibility to run our life, we must life our life to serve. For the time we gave our life over to the care and will of God are the very times when everything effortlessly fell into place.

APRIL 3rd

We Are That Miracle

To say thank you to Spirit for all the good and especially hard times in your life and truly mean it, it is then that you will notice how much you have truly grown. Many times we move along in life taking so many things for granted. Breathing, laughing, walking, speaking out our truths, talking to another person, and many more things. As we look at life and the many things around us through the eyes of gratitude, we begin to truly see just how many amazingly wonderful experiences we have naturally on a daily basis. When you live to serve Spirit, you come to know that a miracle is not simply a random and inconsistent occurrence; it in fact is a constant state of being. Truly we are that miracle, through good times and bad.

APRIL 4th

Beyond The Dark Night

When we think back to the dark nights of our life we can get a clear perspective of just how important it was for us to have those experiences. For those times may very well have been a major turning point in our journey that has placed us upon this exact moment. Every moment is preparation, it is one more step that we will make. Whether we are taking giant leaps or very small baby steps it is carrying us one step further into our incredible journey. Many times we become comfortable and we don't notice that we have taken a holding pattern. We have simply decided to cling tightly to something that no longer serves our highest good. It has been said that when we are pushed to the edge of what we know, it is only then we can move beyond.

APRIL 5th

Still, Quite Rescue

It is in those quite still moments that we feel peace; we feel that connection to Spirit and all that is. In these moments we remember we have all that we will ever need. We are complete and all the things we long for and desire when we are moving to fast will simply settle into place. When we rush around our day and continually live in a state of being all shook up, it is no wonder we feel all jumbled inside. We enter a state of panic and fear and scramble around grasping towards the outer things we think we need. But just as a drowning man must become calm and still, he is able to reach out to his rescue, so as it is with us, we must be still and quite and let Spirit settle into us and we too will find rescue.

APRIL 6th

Words And Actions Of Others

It is often surprising to others the reactions that a person who lives from a place of peace will have to something that feels offensive. When we choose to just let go of something and realize people's actions or words are simply just that, their actions and words. And while Spirit often speaks to us through others, it does not mean that we have to believe that their perception is our truth. For though Spirit speaks through others, he speaks directly to each of us. When we listen to their words or actions from a place of love we can see just what Spirit is saying to us, for it may not be the words or actions that come out but how we perceive them and who we in and how we choose to react.

A PRIL 7th

Do Different To Be Different

Many times it becomes apparent we are participating in a friendship or situation that requires a shift. While it may be hard to accept the solution that will create our highest good, we owe it to our self to honor what is best for us. If we see that a person who claims to be our friend is really being dishonest and spiteful, take a moment to see the situation with love, or where the love is lacking. The way they are behaving really has nothing to do with you; it is the relationship they have with themselves that is reflected through them onto you. Many people have only duplicated the relationships they have been in previously onto new people only to wonder why they are still unhappy. So remember you must do different to be different.

APRIL 8th

Highest Good Or Wishful Thinking?

When you listen to that small still voice it is easy for you to wonder if what you just know is something that is in your highest good or if you are just wishful thinking. Maybe you are experiencing a situation that is not moving at the speed or direction you'd like it to go, so your old reaction is to doubt that what you know to be true will in some way manifest into just what you need. You start to think that your wasting your time and maybe you should move onto something new, but gently remind yourself that you have arrived in the knowing before the other people or circumstances have manifested into your dreams. Be patient and trust that Spirit is the one speaking to you in that still small voice.

APRIL 9th

Do What Makes You Feel Alive

Be observant to the activities of your day. Things seem to perfectly flow together when your thinking is tuned in to the correct frequency. Often times we participate in a lower vibrational thinking and we miss the many small miracles that surround us in every moment we are in. Many times we are mentally not in the moment, while physically we may appear to be doing what we are doing but our mind is else where and really not focused on what we are attempting to do. Other times we simply go through the motions or participate partially in what others want us to do. So why is it we are doing the things we are doing? And most importantly are we really presently doing them? What is the true lesson in going through the motions. Participate in the frequency that makes you feel alive.

APRIL 10th

Free To Choose

The freedom to choose things you'd like to do is one of the best gifts we are given by Spirit. We are able to choose everything we do, what we believe and most importantly who we are. We have all been through many experiences in our lives and while those things help us determine who we will choose to be, it does not define us. For though a situation may cause us pain or happiness it ultimately is an opportunity to grow and learn a valuable lesson in how to love. For in every situation we are free to choose how we will be in that moment. Coming from a place of love will remind us we are free to choose again. Give yourself the freedom you desire for more often than not we are the very barrier we are trying to get around.

A PRIL 11th

Fitting In

Fitting in seems to be simply a matter of perception. What does it mean to fit in? And why is it something we strive to do? When you look at your life and the situations you may be a part of it is usually something within yourself that makes you feel excluded. It is also a place in you that feels unappreciated that creates the wall that will keep other excluded from you. Those are the very same walls that keep you from fitting in with others. The perception we have of ourselves is not always a clear reflection of who we are or how others see us. One of the biggest gifts we can have in life is to remove the very walls we ourselves have chosen to build and notice how perfectly we fit in after all.

A PRIL 12th

Be Open To The Flow

Once you make up your mind it is often hard to see past the expectations you have set. We tend to focus so much on the out come that we can miss other things that are right in front of us. While it is important to set goals and be clear about our intentions it is also necessary to be open to the flow of Spirit. While we may very well be on track to something in our highest good, we should take the time to notice that there are many ways to arrive at the same situation. While the small details may vary it is important to not get stuck on the things that will keep you from feeling productive. Remember that the journey along the way is truly where the beauty lies in reaching what you've made up your mind to accomplish.

APRIL 13th

Serendipity Or Synchronicity

Serendipity and synchronicity are two dear friends that we have no control over. But once they arrive on the scene, life is truly magical. Those moments in time when we truly feel connected inspire us to be more and reach farther than we ever have. There are no accidental meetings or coincidences in life. While things don't always make sense at first, it is in our lessons that we see how things line up, as they should. The universe is always working in our favor to help us live the life we were created to live. The very things we are searching for are also searching for us. So take time to look around you and see how these two friends are working in your life.

APRIL 14th

Walking From The Place Of What You Know

When you walk from the place of what you know, it is then that you feel empowered. You hold your head high and have the confidence to do anything you wish. So why is it that we let fear rob of us of the ability to carry our self in this way all the time? The thought of not knowing something and trying to walk with confidence when you are unsure about something keeps you feeling trapped. This insecurity keeps you feeling "less than." This fear of not being accepted because of what you think you don't know will simply make you feel crazy. So when you get in this cycle, take a minute to stand in a place of what you know so that you can feel your strength, now breath in again and realize that you in fact do know, it is the remembering that brings you peace.

APRIL 15th

The Strength To Overcome Obstacles

Often times our physical body feels challenged or uncomfortable. While our first instinct is to immediately try to fix what is wrong or simply get up and avoid the discomfort. It is in these times that we must challenge our self to see what is really going on by looking at what is going on directly in the face. Do not turn and run. Stand firmly in knowing that you will make it through the situation. You may be challenged in many ways, but you will also discover that you have the strength to overcome any obstacles that may be presented. So whether you choose to avoid the things that make you uncomfortable or you actually seek them out either way you will be presented with another opportunity to learn a new lesson. It is up to you the number of time you will choose to keep repeating the same ones.

APRIL 16th

Relating To Others

It is interesting how others choose to relate and interact with each other. What makes us all so unique is that we each have a different way of showing up in this world. While we feel close to one person and not another it is in the way that we relate that creates our experience. For even those we don't care for and struggle with finding a way to relate, it is another mirror that will show us something new about our self. For the lessons we learn are presented in the forms of others, just as we too are reflecting back to another an opportunity to connect. So in observing the people around you and how they connect to each other will help you understand your own connection.

APRIL 17th

Mend Those Shredded Parts

It is easy to get caught up in the day-to-day activities and lose sight of the things that have the most value. What is it that you hold most dear to your heart? Take a minute to think about the answer. Look back over your day and see how much time you were able to dedicate to those very things. In our fast paced society it gets really easy to have our priorities all over the place. We are often pulled in so many directions all at once that it becomes hard to see that the things that bind us together as a person are coming undone at the seams. So take some time to mend those stressed and fragile parts of yourself by spending some quality time doing the things that you love with the people you value most.

A PRIL 18th

The Peace That Knows

At the very center of our self is that place that knows exactly what we desire to have in our lives. While the mind tries to control what it is we do, it is important to pay attention to how we feel. And while our heart may have some reservations about a situation you can be sure that it is being influenced by the head. While you struggle to find balance between your head and your heart, you will notice that when all is quiet and there is no battle for control going on, it is then that you know. You know because you can feel it and while it makes no sense, it feels pretty fabulous. So remember that everything happens, as it should when Spirit is working in your life.

APRIL 19th

You Are The Answer

It was said one time that you just may be the answer to someone's prayers. Often times we go through our day never noticing the many layers of connections that we have to those around us. We are always exactly where Spirit wants us to be. We meet people and we all learn from each other, without even realizing that we are playing a divine role as we are learning to love our self. How we choose to interact with those around us will determine the quality of how we live our life. Many times we remain stuck in the thoughts that hold us back and we don't feel worthy of being the answer to anything. But Spirit gently reminds us that we in fact are the answer to everything if we come from a place of love.

APRIL 20th

The Newness Of A Moment

It is interesting when we meet new people; we have the perfect opportunity to start the connection off in any way we choose. So why is it that we are so cautious yet eagerly excited all at once? It is in the newness of a moment that we can make the choice to be who we truly are. We can choose to no longer pretend to be something or someone we are not. We can choose to embrace those tender things we know about ourselves and confidently present it to someone new. For they do not know our past, they have not made a judgment about us because they don't know any different. We can create ourselves new everyday and with every choice we make. For in reality everything is always new and exciting if we choose to see it.

APRIL 21st

Lighten Your Load And Let Go

We've all been through things in our life that our so painful we wonder if we will truly ever recover. We wonder if we will make it through alive or even in one piece. As we work through the struggles in our lives we realize that we in fact lose pieces of ourselves and will truly never be the same. But instead of grieving for the pieces we feel are missing we should take some times to notice that Spirit was simply giving us another opportunity to grow and those pieces we tried so hard to hang onto simply had to be removed in order to lighten our load so that we could continue on our journey. The heavy burden that we choose to carry often keeps us from being able to receive the new gifts that are being brought into our life. Spirit will gladly accept those loads if we simply choose to let them go.

APRIL 22nd

Time

Time is a measurable by which many people base everything in their life. How much time needs to go by before we are able to take our next step? When is it okay to do this and how fast should I make a decision? How slow should I go? When and how long will it take me to be ready for what I want? So stop to ponder a minute just what role time plays in your life. We are controlled by calendars, clocks, and made up timetables. None of this truly matters. One person may choose to do something at their own pace. Often our pace is not acceptable by others. So who is aloud to be the judge of what time frame we follow or don't follow? The only measurable you should follow is the one that fills your heart with love and there is no set time that can determine that.

APRIL 23rd

All In Perception

It is truly our perception that creates what we think we
see. But is what we see the truth? For if we take one
simple step to either side of a situation it will provide a
different view completely. While one person may have
the same circumstances that we are having, yet they
completely have an entirely different experience. When
presented with the same thing again and again we can
make a completely new outcome if we choose to see a new
perspective. There are many ways to view our
experiences and while we may see something a certain
way one time does not mean that we will see it the same
way if the opportunity presents itself again. Changing our
perception can be as simple as we believe it can be.
Simply choose to take one small step in any direction.

APRIL 24th

Maintenance Of Your Heart

A good part of our life is spent trying to feel accepted and loved by others. We give away small parts of our self to others in an attempt to fill a hole in their heart, to be something to them that would finally stop their pain. But as time goes by we seldom notice that we our self are shrinking away. We have so few pieces left of our self that we don't even notice how incomplete we have become in an attempt to fulfill another. We all realize that if you gave out all the parts to a car it would no longer run. No one would be so silly to give away the motor to their car, but that is exactly what we do with our very heart and then we try to make excuses about why we thought that would work. Proper maintenance and care of oneself will keep you running.

APRIL 25th

Something Better Is In Store

Love is simply the most amazing feeling. It is the true source of Spirit working in our lives and through our life. The most challenging part is getting beyond those old voices that try to convince you that something so amazing surely can't last. You start to doubt that someone could genuinely feel the same way about you. For in those moments we think back to all those that have moved on without us, and for whatever reasons there may have been, it simply all comes down to something better was in store for you. Your lessons had been presented and you were promoted on to the next level in your development. So just remember that when you are presented with pure love in your life it is Spirits way of showing you just how much you truly are loved, so open your heart to receive and so shall you be able to give.

A PRIL 26th

Take Time

Taking the time to go back a moment to finish up what may have been skipped in haste or simply over looked all together will give you the time to slow down long enough to realize that perhaps your attention has been focused on too many things. We begin to feel overwhelmed and rather than refocus our energies to a few things we can make slow steady progress, we seem to choose to put a little focus on a lot of things and before long it is apparent that we have spread our self too thin to even make a conscious difference on the smallest and simplest tasks. So before you burn out or give up on one of those uncompleted things, remember that all timing is perfect and divine and with our conscious effort we will make progress.

APRIL 27th

What Creates Your Beliefs?

We live our lives based on the beliefs that we hold. But what are your beliefs? Take a minute to see if the beliefs you have been living by are even serving your highest good anymore. Often in our journey we come to realize that the very beliefs we have rearranged our entire existence around turned out to simply be something we were taught to believe and as we learned our lessons we realized that we in fact truly did not believe something, because all along we just simply stopped asking questions and just thought someone else knew more than we did. While it is very important to have beliefs it is even more important to have your own. For some beliefs may very well be what is holding you back. When we are searching for our truth it is then we come to understand and appreciate the choice we have in creating our beliefs.

APRIL 28th

The Opinion That Matters Is Yours

True confidence is found when you no longer focus on what others think of you. Many times we feel less than we truly are and we expect that others feel this way about us because that is how we are feeling about our self. When you do things in your life that bring you peace and happiness, you start to focus more on what you're feeling and less on what others may or may not think about you. Usually we admire the strong and confident people but on occasion we try too hard to get their approval and we become a person who appears to lack the very things that are drawing us to them. So remember to breath and be yourself and realize that the one person's opinion of who you are that matters is yours.

APRIL 29th

Speak Up

Speaking up to others about how you feel is very important. Sometimes we think others will simply do the right thing because that is what we would do. It just doesn't occur to us that we may be operating on a completely different frequency then they are. Frustration with others will start to build up unless you speak up. Others cannot and will not read your mind; they will not know where you are coming from unless you tell them. Honor your relationships enough to have the courage to communicate whether it is in words or action, and extend the trust and faith that you will be heard. We are each responsible for only our half of the friendship. Holding things in is holding back and we must all be willing to live our lives full out so that we can experience our life to the fullest.

A PRIL 30th

You Can't Out Run Yourself

Running from things that seem hard often leads to a really tough reaction to break. Some of us spend so much time changing things and staying busy so we can avoid getting hurt. We look at our circumstances and think that if we simply walk away that we will no longer have to deal with the painful parts. So we get a new job, a different car, a new lover or anything that will occupy our time. We develop a habit or addiction that will cover it up or make it disappear. Then we finally realize that no matter how far or how long we run we have gone nowhere. For the problems we run from or the hurt we try to avoid by living life in a small safe way always seem to show up again. Maybe with a new face or a clever disguise but we cannot run from our self forever.

MAY 1st

Attitude Of Gratitude

Living your life from pure gratitude will help you see things in a whole new light. Having a positive outlook on any situation will greatly increase your feeling of peace. You will be able to find your center and remain calm and know that everything works out. When we allow our self to get caught up in the drama and the negative feelings we take the risk of spinning out of control and fear begins to show up. With every breath you take and every beat of your heart there is a moment to practice gratitude. We have spent enough of our life living from the opposite side of the coin only to appreciate things when we have lost them. Often times we don't even notice all that we have to be grateful for. So make your attitude one of gratitude.

M AY 2nd

Take Action

Sometimes we are so overwhelmed that logic doesn't even make sense. We think so much about how we might do something better or differently and then we find that we have exhausted our self completely and in our tired frustration we leave out the most important part. Action! We decide to do nothing. We will think about it again later. Then we revisit the same old things again only to realize that we have not accomplished anything except to waste more valuable time putting off something that we have decided makes no sense when truly it simply requires action that we are hesitating to take. So instead of putting it off until later be still long enough to seek the guidance that is seeking you to take action.

MAY 3rd

Things Don't Have To Make Sense

Sometimes things don't seem to make any sense at all, yet in the exact same moment it all perfectly fits like the piece of a puzzle and in your heart it makes complete sense. We often seek the approval of another to follow through on something that is calling our heart. Spirit works in so many mysterious ways that it can often overwhelm us. So rather than allow the moments to pass us by we should realize that everything is perfect as it is. In that moment we know that this is really all there is. When our heart is filled with the love of Spirit we can let go of the illusion that things need to make sense, for our perception may be blinding us from the true reality.

MAY 4th

Your Gifts Are On The Way

The anticipation of an event or situation in your life you are looking forward to, can often overwhelm you with that same feeling you used to get when you still believed in Santa. Santa would bring you some amazing gifts that you'd been hoping for, and the excitement of knowing exactly what day and time you could count on this arrival would just leave you unable to sleep and imagining all the possibilities you'd have once you received all the things you'd been hoping for. So why don't we realize that every day is a new opportunity for us to receive the many gifts that Spirit has in store for us? So think back to when you believed without question and you just knew that your gifts were on the way.

MAY 5th

Another Option

What seems to be obvious to one person may be completely unclear to another. Often times we are so immersed in our own problems that we truly cannot see beyond the limits of our thinking in that moment. We forget or simply refuse to see another option. We have made up our mind that we have to be right or continue to dwell on why things are going so wrong in the first place. In our attempts to seek validation we go from one person to another crying out all the while they are not really making us feel any better. And then finally we realize that if we took a step back and removed our self from the situation we may have a more clear perspective. For the truth lies in our openness to change our perspective. It is then we can see what may have been there all along.

MAY 6th

What Is It We See Or Don't See?

It is scary to walk blindly through a pitch-black room. Or is it? One may say the same thing about walking to the edge of what we have always known and then pushing one step further into the unknown. Many wonderful opportunities are available to us in every new moment. So what makes it scary when we cannot see? So we may trip, fall and bump up against unexpected things. Sometimes we choose to avoid the things we see simply because it looks to challenging. But is it any less challenging then what we don't see? We may be more accepting of new experiences if we simply choose not to label it based on what we think we already know about it based on what we can or cannot see.

MAY 7th

Divine Timing

It is amazing when you notice how appropriately the universe coordinates timing. Everything happens in the divine timing of a higher natural order. Sometimes the smaller things we have been putting off will pile up until we are sent a very large clear signal that our attention is required now, not on our own timing, but in accordance to the appropriate timing. One that fits into the divine order and moves us one step closer to realizing that we are often our own worst problem. For sometimes the best thing we can do is step aside out of our own way and allow life to flow, as it should and when it should.

MAY 8th

A Divine Fit

The part we play in the life of others is the very same part
we play in our own. Whether we choose to see it or not is
half of our problem. Many times we don't give our self
enough credit for the value we bring to our world. We
certainly fail to notice what we bring to those around us.
If we stop judging our actions based on everyone else's
expectations we will be able to realize that we are all
connected to each other and collectively we are all
designed to fit together to bring a divine value to the
experience of the journey of our lives. Sometimes the part
we play for one may be small and for another we may be
one of their greatest teachers, so reflect on the people in
your life and you will see just how perfectly we all work
together to teach each other.

MAY 9th

A Memory Or An Experience

Life changes so quickly that when you're in the middle of something you don't realize that in a flash it will all be different. Appreciating the moment and the circumstances of your life each day will help you see the value of just how many amazing experiences Spirit brings into your life. While we are feeling joy or sorrow in that moment we can remind our self that this too shall pass. And once again an ordinary possibly uneventful day will be added to the other memories we may or may not even remember. So whether you choose to remember something or simply experience it and move on, you will forever be changed in some way. Each day and every moment is the next baby step we take on our journey of life.

MAY 10th

A Peaceful Connection

Sitting outside is one of the easiest ways to feel connected to Spirit. You can simply sit and listen to the many things around you. You can watch the people going by and while they smile and go by they too are on their way to somewhere. The birds sing and fly around, they too are doing something. Being the silent observer who simply acknowledges how everything really is connected requires very little action on our part to feel connected. For while we may not be going where the people are going or doing what the birds are doing, we are still very much a part of what is going on. For this moment is another beautiful opportunity to simply do nothing while experiencing a peaceful connection.

MAY 11th

Be True To Who You Are

What image have you been showing to others? Often times when we are searching for who we really are, we go through different stages of how it is we show up. Many times we are frustrated with others for how they may be viewing us. But what part are we playing? Many times we will act like someone we are not because we feel like that is what others expect us to be. But do they really expect that from us or is it simply what we have assumed they are expecting? Does it really matter if we meet another's expectations at the risk of not even being true to who we really are? We may have many images that bind us to ego and keep us from experiencing who we really are. Be yourself for that is who God created you to be. It's ok to learn as you go. That's what life is all about.

M AY 12th

Let Go And Let God

Learning to let go and let God is something that most of us have heard all our lives. Many of us even claim to be doing that. But are we truly letting go and letting God? It is a little more challenging than it sounds. We often think we are capable of doing things our self and rarely do we let others in. But name one thing you can do without Spirit? You can't even take one breath or beat one beat of your heart. Maybe you don't know the specifics of how that deed works but you have come to trust that it will happen. So why is it so hard to trust God to do all the other things. Certainly none are more important than the very activities that keep you alive and you trust God to do that. So put it all into perspective and you will see that it is easier than you've made it.

MAY 13th

Love Your Self

One of the greatest gifts we are given by Spirit is free will. We have the ability to make any decision at any moment. Often times in our greatest need we make decisions that hurt others and greatly destroy our self. The guilt and shame we feel for a poor decision often leads to the most severe punishment imaginable inflicted on us by our self. Rather than trying to act lovingly towards the situation and our self we simply feel like we don't deserve forgiveness much less the respect or second chance of those that love us. By remembering that we have the freedom to choose differently we can be different. For if others can love us shouldn't we then also try to love our self?

MAY 14th

Take Responsibility For Your Life

Finding the strength and courage to take responsibility for your own life and decisions can be a slow and steady process. When we learn to do this we can find peace with our self and with other people. To discover that the actions of another really have very little to do with us can be both frustrating as well as a relief. We feel like if we could have done more or been more then maybe they would have done this or perhaps not done that. It really all comes down to the same thing, we do what we do because we are choosing to and so do others. When you do things for your own well being it is a natural flow to the others and even the world.

M AY 15th

Stop Having Both Sides Of The Conversation

I have often been told to stop having both sides of the conversation. I often think I am simply just trying to think things through so that I can be prepared. But prepared for what really? We are all prepared for anything that may arise. We simply have numerous opportunities to extend enough trust to another to give them the opportunity to speak for themselves. To decide for themselves how they choose to show up in the experience. Fear often leads us to believe that things will not go as we hope, but what we forget to realize is that things may possibly go better than we could ever have imagined. Our fear based thinking limits the boundaries we have set on our self and keeps us from experiencing the true gift of Spirit.

MAY 16th

Nurture The Respect

Listening to others is the first step to learning to trust. To listen without judgment and show genuine concern and respect for where another is coming from can be healing for all involved. Sharing their story and struggles as well as triumphs can shed a lot of light on what a true gift a friendship can be. There are no secret tricks to being a great friend and many times a genuine friendship can bring our greatest challenges. For a true friend will not simply tell us what we want to hear, they are going to help us dig deeper by questioning us when we seem to be complacent. But the main ingredient is respect. For respect gains trust and with trust comes honesty, so look around at your friends and nurture that respect.

MAY 17th

Projecting Our Fears Onto Others

Often times we project our fears and issues on to the people around us. Many of these times we don't even realize that is what we are doing. But when the challenge to grow comes, we realize what our fears are and that we are actually using them to hide behind and holding others responsible for things they had nothing to do with. These people are simply a gift in our life to help us notice that we indeed have an opportunity to work through some of our issues, but we must first take responsibility for the issues and then make a conscious decision to make different choices out of love, trust and forgiveness, not only to those that may have caused us pain, but also to our self for continuing to carry that pain so long.

M AY 18th

Drawn To Another

On our journey we find our self-drawn to another, perhaps it's spiritually, physically, emotionally or mentally. Sometimes it's on every level and the intensity is overwhelming, exciting and confusing all at once. Your mind struggles for control while your heart steps up and refuses to shut down. While this person guides you to new places you feel the amazing connection that feels safer than anything you've ever allowed in, but you also feel the fear and confusion. You can feel the battle going on between your head and heart as you search for balance and face the lessons that are coming up. For when you connect on all levels it is the perfect divine opportunity to trust Spirit, while you work through this and allow yourself to completely love another as yourself.

MAY 19th

Trusting Yourself, Trusting Another

When we are still long enough to at least trust that inner voice, we will notice just how much unnecessary torment we put our self through with our inability to trust others. We get caught up in the worldly ideas of what we think we need or want or worse yet in what others may expect of us. We often tend to take things personal and react to the actions of another, thinking they were about us. Nothing that another chooses really has as much to do with us, as our ego would like to think. Our choices have everything to do with us, so once we learn to start trusting our self then we will realize that it is safe to trust another. It is in that trust we will find the peace we seek.

MAY 20th

The Energies Of Love

It has been said that when you love others it is really you loving the experience of yourself when you are with that person. Much comfort can be found in those words. The love you are feeling is not coming from them to you; it is simply extending out from you to them. The energies that meet and mix are nothing less than magical. When one person is not coming from a place of love it can often leave us feeling depleted in our efforts to achieve the feeling we think to be love. When we label love and try to define how it should look and feel then we are not being true. For if we are love as Spirit created us to be then there are no words to define it, nor energies to deplete it.

M AY 21st

Letting Go And Walking Away

Letting go of a person you love can be difficult. It is in those times that we must remember that we are not alone. Nor can we find the strength to walk away on our own. Often our hearts long for the happy days we once shared with the other person and we sometimes ignore and accept all of the inappropriate behavior in hopes that we can return to what once was. In the realization that we will never be able to return to those days we learn to accept what is in this day. When we come to accept that the relationship we have with the other person may not be in our highest good anymore we must learn to bless the situation and love our self enough to trust Spirit and follow the next step which may be to walk away.

MAY 22nd

The Other Side Of Devastation

When what appears to be a devastating event takes place in your life it is often difficult to see what positive outcomes could be possible. Choices often have to be made in order to move forward. While one may struggle in the stages between anger, fear and many other emotions it is in the still quiet moments that we can find hope, courage and strength that will carry us through another lesson. As we move forward in our recovery we learn to reclaim our life, we are reminded of what is truly important to us. Priorities shift and we learn to appreciate the very basics, those same things that we have come to take for granted. Open your heart to the possibilities that Spirit is bringing forth in your life. For devastation is simply the other side of a new beginning.

MAY 23rd

Start By Speaking Up

Speaking your truth to those around you is the most important quality a person can have. And while others may not agree with you, they will have the opportunity to get another perspective. Every person has the freedom to choose their own values, morals and beliefs. When a person speaks of things that are important to them it is a way of connecting to others. We are being trusted by that person. We are not expected to agree but we should respect their truth and appreciate the opportunity to connect on a deeper level. When you hold back on what you believe to be true for yourself you miss out on possibilities that you may have never even dreamed of. It all starts by speaking up.

M AY 24th

The Results Of Control

Sometimes the most unexpected things will happen. You can never really plan these types of occurrences. Often we get stuck in how we think things should be or we simply are too angry and disappointed that we can't see that something larger than we are is in action. We get frustrated even more when things seem to be out of our control. But if we slow down enough we may notice the results we have achieved in our past when we were in control. Trusting that Spirit will be with us through every lesson is a great first step in letting go. We grasp so tightly to our circumstances that we fail to notice we in fact are draining the very life out of what it is we are hanging on so tightly to control. And then it happens, we notice by letting go that the unexpected miracles that have been trying to enter our life have the freedom to flow into our world and our heart.

MAY 25th

Challenges Inspire Us To Move Beyond

Along our journey we encounter many different situations. We meet many people and we experience an unlimited amount of opportunities that will not only challenge us but inspire us to move above and beyond what we thought possible. A lot of thought and energy are put towards what we think will bring solutions or outcomes that we think are favorable. We spend way too much time judging and labeling things as bad or good. But who is really the judge of that? What at first glance may seem to be a horrible experience may in fact be the turning point in the road that helps you get to where you really need to be. While we do not have a detailed road map of our journey, we can be sure that all roads lead to Spirit and if we simply trust, it is then that we realize that our heart is the only map we really need.

MAY 26th

Finding Closure

Many people think that closure means a situation will be resolved and we will be free to move forward. It has also been viewed as the end of circumstances that have been emotionally crippling you. Often time's people get stuck in the healing process because we are under the impression that all parties must come to the closure together. When we get quiet and listen to the voice of Spirit we often discover that we are all in different places and while one person may be able to find closure in a relationship or circumstance with the other person, some people will have to do the work to find peace and the closure they are looking for within themselves. Sometimes closure is found when we find our courage to take back the power we gave to others and realize that we have the right to choose what is in our highest good and we have the choice to move on.

MAY 27th

Take Hold Of What's In Front Of You

It is easy to become rattled by the distractions of the things going on around us. And while we may know that we are safe and the situation is secure we often have a hard time getting out of our head. When we have formed an opinion or an idea about a situation we often times feel uncomfortable when we are out of our normal routine. But if we take time to be in the moment and appreciate the steps and motivation of what brought us to this point we will find safety and security in knowing that we are not alone, and we are exactly where we need to be in that moment. We are having the experience we were meant to have so let go of the discomfort that has you rattled and take hold of what is right in front of you and know that you are safe.

MAY 28th

Clarity Of The Heart

It is interesting that we may choose a situation that has clear rules, no strings and the perfect opportunity to stay detached. We learn to accept it for what it is. Nothing more or nothing less. We appreciate that while we are involved in our experience we are also very clear on why it is necessary to honor each moment as it is. We understand that the reason we have chosen this lesson is that we will not become delusional about the potential possibilities of where this might lead. For when we appreciate that it is not intended to have an expected outcome we have surrendered the inevitable disappointment that would follow. When Spirit is in charge it becomes clear that a higher order is at work so there is no need to question, because without delusion comes clarity, clarity of the heart.

MAY 29th

Do What Makes You Happy

When we stop worrying about everyone else and what others are doing, we give our self the freedom to do what makes us happy. We understand that we are not responsible for the choices that another person makes. We choose for our self and we respect the choices of others. We learn to value the sacredness that comes with the experiences we are so blessed to have when we open our heart to fully enjoy how it feels to finally put our self first. For whatever we choose to do in our life that brings us happiness, it will also bring happiness to others, for they will have the benefit of experiencing us as we truly are. When you live your life for others with no regard for yourself it is easy to lose track of what you so truly deserve.

MAY 30th

What Is Right For You

Who is to decide what is right or wrong for you? While Spirit always guides you to your higher good, it is up to you to be willing to unlearn or perhaps relearn a way of thinking. It matters not so much what others think about your choices, as it matters how you feel about them. What may be unthinkable for some may actually be the perfect lesson you need to learn. We are all at different stages of learning in this life and it is important to maintain your center as you walk forward on the path you are meant to travel. For on your journey you will encounter many people, with many ideas on what you need. But for the most part you will realize that people are not so sure what they need for themselves so how do they know what it is that you need?

M AY 31st

Divinity Of Spirit In Us All

Connections made between people can transport you to a sacred space. The trust and intimacy that creates the connection will help you learn more about the unchartered territory of who you really are. Many connections are made with others over our lifetime. All are unique and essential to our own soul's development. While we may walk through our life with a lot of different ideas about the concepts of love, relationships and how to live, we realize that every situation is another way to learn to love our self. Making a connection with another that makes you feel alive is simply an example of the ever-present grace of Spirit in your life. For Spirit knows what inspires you and when you step out of your own way you are free to connect to the divinity of Spirit in others and they too can connect with you.

JUNE 1st

Be Proactive Instead Of Reactive

The beauty of choice helps you realize that you can decide to be proactive in what it is that you want by taking action rather than being reactive to what others try to force upon you. When you have courage and strength in yourself you see things more clearly and you are able to make choices that will be healthy for you. Often times we make irrational decisions based on our emotions. We may feel angry or rejected and rather than come from a place of love we react from fear. We lash out in an attempt to hide how we are feeling So rather than react, simply decide what you would like to see happen in your life and make a proactive choice to take action.

JUNE 2nd

Embrace The Differences

It is in the moments of complete opposition with someone we love and are close to, that we can clearly see the parts of our self that are calling to us to be healed. One person may excel at communication while the other chooses to use other non-verbal forms to connect. Both feeling uncomfortable with their own interpretation of what is going on with the other or perhaps within themselves. The true beauty is found in the simple reality that these two have created the most amazing opportunity to expand their own hearts and understanding if only they choose to be grateful for the lessons that come with the complete trust and acceptance of not only themselves but each other and to embrace the differences with the connection of that love drew them together.

JUNE 3rd

Teaching You To Grow

As we are growing up we are a part of a family. We spend a great deal of our time watching and learning from those that are around us the most. Things are done a certain way and at that age we don't really know anything different. We simply do as we were taught to do. It isn't until much later in our life that we realize that everything can be done in a variety of ways. It doesn't make them right or wrong. While we often get stuck in the things we do not have anymore, it is far more important to know that what you may have barely tolerated would be a welcome change as time goes by. So it really doesn't matter your age or how you were raised, it is important to look around and see all the wonderful blessings that are teaching you to grow.

JUNE 4th

It Will All Work Out Just As It Should

When you're frustrated with situations in your life, it can be difficult to see the lesson that is at work. You become attached to the outcome that you think you want, while all along you are really unsure of the route you are supposed to take. You try to think about all the solutions and options that might make everything work out. While you may be torn on your decision, certain actions or inactions of others may make it easier for you to finally walk away or set a major change into place. While you may not see the higher plan at work, you can rest assured that whether you make yourself crazy with all the stress or simply relax, it will all work out just as it should.

JUNE 5th

Endless Possibilities

We often hide ourselves in situations or relationships that are safe. One person is often emotionally unavailable for something that could be more, but what you have seems to meet certain needs. You know going into it what the boundaries are and that it will simply be what it is. And while you may learn the importance of being in the moment you begin to master not becoming delusional with what could be, for you know that with all the limitations it cannot be more than it is. And while you tell yourself that your ok with everything, that small voice keeps asking you if you are hiding from putting yourself out there. Always remember that when Spirit is involved, what may seem one way can really be anyway in a simple flash. Know that possibilities are endless in every single situation even the safe predictable ones.

JUNE 6th

Arrive In Your Glory

We take some time to rest and slow down enough to find our center. We are able to relax to the point of letting go of all the thoughts and concerns we may have been focusing on. When we decide that no thought or action and the many voices that are calling for attention all need to be still, it is in those moments that we truly are able to experience peace. Our breathing steadies and time is suspended. For we understand in the moment that all is exactly as it should be, with our without our effort. For the result we achieve may be arrived at in many ways. We may discover we can show up to our own life exhausted and out of breathe as easily as we can arrive in all our magnificent glory.

JUNE 7th

The Quality Of Our Days

When one is faced with a difficult life changing choice, it is important to take a step back and look at your options carefully. Pause and listen to the still small voice that has always been there showing the way. That faint whisper at times you could barely hear from the screaming voices that were demanding your attention. All the while you were drawn to that silent comforting feeling that was present when that voice spoke. As we walk our path to Spirit we discover that we have the ability to heighten our senses, to turn up our hearing, to tune out the chaos, to open our mind and heart completely and let Spirit guide us to what we could do in this moment. For often times we realize that it is not in the quantity of our days here but in the quality of our days that make our life joyous.

JUNE 8th

Respect Others For The Part They Have Played

Many times people try so hard to please another that it often results in pushing them away. Someone may feel hurt and rejected when all along it is simply working out exactly as it should. In those moments we are able to look at the situation and realize that the best solution is to let go of the expectations of not only the other person but of yourself as well. Taking care of you may include walking away. It may later include a willingness to forgive and simply accept the other person for who they are and the experience for the lessons you have learned. While you may not really truly know the effect or influence you may have had in another's life, one thing you can be sure of is that Spirit provided all the involved the opportunity to make a difference. So respect others for the part they have played in your life.

JUNE 9th

Accept The Life You Are Meant To Have

What might the future hold for you as you make choices that will help you shape your life? It is such a blessing to know that absolutely anything is possible. If you can dream it, then you can become it. Many times we get so overwhelmed in the details that we limit our self. We sometimes box our self into a corner, we allow the external world to dictate our options. Our power is drained from us by circumstances and situations that simply have no business playing such a large undeserving role in our life. When we harness that divine power that is within us we can move forward to the life that Spirit wants us to have. For limitations and lack are not in our highest good, nor are they the perfect end result. So simply accept the life you are meant to have and know that you deserve it.

JUNE 10th

Finding The Balance

There is a part of each of us that moves from the desire to be free from the limitations and boundaries often contained in a relationship with another to the even stronger desire of connection to a special someone. The perfect relationship can evolve when it is first obtained within yourself. When you live your life from a peaceful place you become willing to give in ways that will attract that same love right back to you. You will find that the honoring of one's space and speaking up for your own needs will help you maintain that desired state of freedom. One does not need to remain alone in order to honor those feelings within them. When two people can find balance of these feelings within them self it is then that you will be able to create that connection with another.

JUNE 11th

Go Forward In Your Day

When we wake up in the morning we sometimes start thinking about all the things that we need to do in that day. If we first wake up and remind ourselves of all the things we have to be grateful for it sets the tone of our day. Leave some room in your day to be spontaneous. Create the space to allow the unexpected blessings that will come your way this day. For if you become so focused on all the things you have to do and just exactly how you will do them, you will lose the magic of adventure. Know that you will accomplish all that you must in this day but you will do so without all the unnecessary pressure that you tend to put upon yourself. So go forward in your day and enjoy the miracles that will occur.

JUNE 12th

We All Make A Difference

It is truly amazing when you realize the difference you make in this world. The activities of your day have an effect not only on you and your world but the entire world in which you live in. Collectively we have all come to this experience to make a difference, and while we learn our lessons as we travel our path, it is those lessons that make us who we are. For with each experience and lesson comes a knowledge gained that will be needed along the way. You may not feel like you are making a difference but when you do the best you can and respect others around you, you will realize that together we all can and do make a significant difference and we all need to work together, for that is when you will be able to feel the impact that our actions have on our world.

JUNE 13th

Genuine In Your Intentions

For so many years you may have bent over backwards to please other people. You give in to demands that are not only unreasonable but completely inappropriate to even consider in the first place. Yet you comply and often times jeopardize your own well-being because you truly believe that it will make a difference to the other person. Not only did it not really make a difference but they didn't even appreciate the effort. They found fault in how you did it rather than be grateful that you were able to do it in the first place. So on top of all this you are left feeling defeated and taken for granted. You even go as far as beating yourself up for being such a push over. Take a minute to love yourself through the lesson and the fact that you were genuine in your intentions. Put your own well being first and know that Spirit has a plan and will never be disappointed in your efforts.

JUNE 14th

Space to Experience The Results

Sometimes it can be discouraging to watch people you love go through things that could go in such a different direction, if only they would look at the situation from a different perspective. Many times a person is so focused on all the negative aspects of their circumstances that they remain in the problem. They are unable and usually unwilling to choose a different approach. Rather than try to list some possible solutions and different approaches they simply amplify the very things that are bothering them the most. You wonder why they have even asked you for your opinion or feed back when it falls on unopened ears. Be patient and realize that they are not yet to where you are in a simplified understanding. Listen to them, be honest, but be willing to give them their space to experience the results that will occur with their decisions. Most importantly remember that this is their lesson not yours.

JUNE 15th

Something Bigger

There are those moments in your life that you just know that something bigger than you dreamed is coming true. You have spent time doing things and have felt like this was worth doing. Very rarely do you have such a deep knowing that your body just shifts into a state of preparation and you realize that this is the life you have been working towards. You're not quite sure of the exact details and actions that will occur or even how you will remain patient and proceed in the divine unfolding timing. You can see the big picture and while parts may be unclear you just know that this is what you have been being prepared for. Allow Spirit to work through you and honor the ways in which Spirit works through those around you and things will simply fall into place.

JUNE 16th

Give Yourself Permission

Giving yourself permission to have an experience because that is what your heart says is the first step towards breaking through your own self imposed walls. Often times our head tells us that we should not even bother and then the internal war begins. Our mind starts coming up with all the reasons and excuses why we should not move forward. And then that same mind starts justifying why we should move forward, back and forth in an internal battle of wills. Once some agreement has been debated and the exhaustion has gained control we realize how simple it could have been to simply trust that Spirit is at work here and that is why our heart has spoken up. Trust that this experience is another step towards discovering your true self. When you choose to skip the battle you will be able to appreciate the opportunity that this experience will bring. So embrace it with an energetic heart.

JUNE 17th

The State Of Pure Innocent Love

Look back over the years and you will see just how much you have grown into a person with an expanded awareness of what love really is. All the events in your life whether they were painful or exhilarating have brought you right to where you are. Early in our lives we know and can feel love; it is simply our natural state of being. As we grow and make choices we experience many things that move us into a feeling that does not really represent a true love. Fear will cause us to manipulate and try to control others to get that feeling we desire with another. As we get closer to Spirit and start discovering who we really are we outgrow those old ways. We are willing to give our self in the ways that Spirit has intended. It is then we return to the state of pure innocent love, that same state we were born with.

JUNE 18th

Spirit Will Bring You Through

In the experiences we have in our journey called life we often encounter lessons that seem so unbearable that you wonder if you will make it though. And while you may lose track of time and struggle to maintain a sense of sanity, all the while you know your faith will see you through this and you will indeed make it. You dig deep into yourself, look for the tools you've collected along the way, but as you feel your heart aching you simply do not have enough strength on your own to lift yourself up. Then you decide to allow yourself to feel the pain rather than pretend it doesn't hurt this bad. You surrender to that voice that reminds you that you are not alone and you find peace in knowing that the love of Spirit will bring you through this.

JUNE 19th

Focus On The Good

As you wake up each day you are reminded that this day can be anything you make it. When you look around and acknowledge all the things you have to be grateful for you notice that the universe keeps bringing you even more wonderful blessings to add to the list. It is when we look for the good in every situation the bad doesn't take over. For what we focus on is what seems larger than it may need to be. So why not focus on the good? It is all in how we perceive things that will change our perspective. When we learn not to judge things as good or bad, but to accept that things just are, then we will start to notice that some of the best things appear to come from a situation that may not seem so great. Life is in constant movement to greatness.

JUNE 20th

Honor And Respect Yourself

We are all on our own separate yet united journey. While what we do may hurt or help others, it is important to remember that you must honor and respect yourself. For when you are patient and loving with yourself you will be able to show that towards others. As we grow and often realize we have made our life complicated, we start to understand that when we live to please others we set our self up for failure. Because no matter what you do in life you will come to learn that you must take responsibility for your actions and decisions you have made. And while we live out the consequences of our choices we find Gods grace in all we do when we love our self enough to forgive others, and ourselves on our journey to discovering the peace that is within us.

JUNE 21st

Sing Your Song

Music is the language that inspires every living being. The words in a song can touch your heart in so many ways. It can transport you into another time, a different place. When you open your heart you will notice the music that is all around you, the chirping of a bird, the raindrops from the sky, the whistling in the wind. It is then you make the connection; it is the beating of your heart, the rhythm of your soul expressing itself through everything that is. The universal language we all know and feel is love, so when we express the music in our heart we understand that it comes in many forms, it is expressed in many ways. So sing your song and enjoy the symphony of your life.

JUNE 22nd

Free To Go

Sometimes people have been hurt so badly by things that have happened in their life that they seem to close down. A wall is built to keep others out, to help them feel safe once again. They stay to themselves never to venture out from their guarded fortress. Communication becomes a tool that is amplified only inside their own head. And while they may think it is harmless and safe to keep so guarded they fail to notice they have built their own prison, a prison from which there is no easy way out. How do you get past the one person that keeps denying your freedom? You get angry and scared but then you look up and see the light that is shining in. You feel your heart start to soften and you peek out to see that you are free to go, safer in fact outside those big walls.

JUNE 23rd

Searching For What Is Within You

We find things to occupy our time. We stay busy searching for the acceptance of others. We look to people for understanding while all along we are avoiding those dark and tender places that are calling out for healing. Hoping we will create an experience that will give us the space to feel loved, to feel appreciated and mostly to feel safe. For when we get tired and worn down emotionally and are unsure of what to do next, we long for a safe place to lay our head and pour out our heart. When what and who we have been looking for has been right in front of us all along. We were too busy to see them, too scared to open up. But once you have enough faith to just let go you will see that everything you have been searching for has been within you all along.

JUNE 24th

Not Our Place To Interfere

The relationships between the people we love around us give us the opportunity to learn even more about our self and why it is so important to remember that it is not our place to interfere with what goes on. We think that because we love them and they are in our life that we have some sort of say. It is tempting to try and fix everything for someone and give them advice based on what you would do. Everyone has their own unique connection and no two relationships are the same. So what may be best in one scenario may be the worst in another. We do not know the lessons of our self or others, so it would be foolish to try and interfere with what may be a very important lesson that has to be played out in a particular way. So trust that all happens, as it should.

JUNE 25th

Love Of Spirit In The Truest Sense

Events and circumstances happen in our lives that help us define who we are and what really matters. There are those moments when they very things you have dreamed of seem to be happening all around you. The overwhelming feeling of gratitude is flowing through you and you instantly know that this is truly Gods grace working in your life. You don't see any problems, feel any discomfort. In fact things flow as smoothly as running water. Every moment has brought you right to where you are. And while challenges will once again rise up and demand your attention you can rest in knowing that it is all part of the overall plan, for without those challenging moments we would not truly understand the beauty of those divine opportunities to feel the love of Spirit in the truest sense.

JUNE 26th

A Divine Experience To Expand Your Heart

Sometimes it is hard to not take things personal when you are disappointed with the words or actions of another. Perhaps you have become more concerned with thinking you know more about what is better for them than they do. You can't understand why something that seems logical and perfect isn't obvious to them. It may very well be that others think the same way about you. Sometimes we just don't see the same things in the same way. Take a deep breath and remind yourself that Spirit is actively at work in your life. And while you may feel one way about how something may need to go, don't be discouraged because the outcome will surely be better than you ever imagined and the unpredictable path you may travel will be the divine experience that will expand your heart.

JUNE 27th

Enjoy Where You Are

Look all around you and you will see the many small signs that despite what you might think, you are right on track with where you should be. We tend to get caught up in where we wish we were and often frustrated for where we are. Perhaps there are other things you need to learn before you are ready to be in different situations confirmations and the reassurance from Spirit that all things unfold in a divine timing. Our timing is not so relevant in the bigger scheme of things. We live in a society of instant gratification where we often miss out on many great opportunities and experiences due to our own impatience. In our effort to rush straight to our desires we forget to trust that Spirit knows exactly what we need and when we are ready to handle having it. So enjoy where you are.

JUNE 28th

Vital Connections

In our connections with other people we learn so much about our self. While one friendship may spin you out of control another may be the one that reminds you how to keep your head straight. Different people will play various parts in your life. One person cannot fulfill every aspect or need you may have in your life. Each of your connections is a vital part of keeping the harmony and balance that is going to bring you a sense of fulfillment. The important thing to remember is that our friends will mirror back to us the many qualities that we may or may not be able to see. Spirit is the true source of all and once we remember that we are here by a divine appointment we are able to appreciate the unique relationships that we have in our lives.

JUNE 29th

The Universe Has Lined Up Your Dreams

We meet people in our lives and have an instant connection to them. Things just seem to flow naturally. It's as if no effort is required at all to feel harmony and gratitude to be around them. And while you can't explain what you feel, you just simply know in your heart that you love these people. You know that your presence in each other's lives will make a lasting difference. And while circumstance and timing may seem to be off at times you realize that patience and love will bring the most amazing experiences when the timing is right. The universe has lined up your dreams for you; it is up to you to believe that you are exactly where you need to be and whom you need to be with.

JUNE 30th

Grateful To Feel Something

When you are blind sided it is often challenging to react with so many feelings coming to the surface all at once. You have the mind telling you one thing, the heart saying something else and a whole host of feelings trying to take center stage. When you take a moment to say and do nothing, it is then that the raging emotions will settle just enough to allow some clarity to rise to the surface. While you may be holding back tears and grasping for breathe in what feels like a stabbing. All the while every old pattern you have is fighting to take over and simply settle this quickly, painlessly and heartlessly. So instead of shutting down because you feel wounded, be grateful in the realization that you are feeling something. So allow the love that created your feeling to guide you through this.

JULY 1st

A Painful Separation

More often than not the things that cause us pain are simply not even about us. It is about the meaning and expectation we have attached to the circumstances that cause our painful downfall. When we detach from the painful situations we are facing and take some ownership of the part we play we can then see that if we look at the situation with love we will be able to show not only respect to our self but to the entire situation. What is really causing us pain? Generally it is disappointment or fear. Fear of not being loved or accepted. Thinking you're being rejected when someone pulls away. But we are being loved and can never really be rejected. We simply choose to separate from Spirit in that moment and that is what is causing our pain.

JULY 2nd

The Same Lesson

We draw into our experience the opportunity to heal. We meet people that will perfectly reflect the very things we need to work on. While the details will change and so will the people, the lessons will become clear. We may recreate a multitude of ways to practice the same lesson. Maybe we are only learning a small part of the overall teaching. Perhaps we were not ready to learn the entire lesson in just one experience. With each new experience we also gain the ability to progress forward in the pace that we will be able to cope with. Many times our ego will cause us to take on more than we need to at that moment. Be patient with yourself as you learn these lessons even when you feel like it is the same one over and over. For it is exactly what you need and at the pace you need it. Trust Spirit as you go.

JULY 3rd

Everything Really Does Happen For A Reason

There are no chance meetings, no coincidences and certainly no mistakes. In the divine order of life the universe will provide us with many opportunities. Things will line up, as they should. Now on the surface it may appear that everything is chaotic and not going as planned or it will simply fall into place as you dreamed it would. So what's really going on here? Our perception of what we think the outcome should be is what causes us to label the experience as good or bad. But time and patience will show us that once again everything really does happen as it should and according to the divine plan. Everything really does happen for a reason. So as you travel along your path, learn to be grateful for every opportunity to grow and heal.

JULY 4th

Happy Independence Day

Happy Independence Day! What a gift it is to know we all have the freedom to be independent. While we all follow many rules or laws of the communities we live in, it all really goes back to the basic and simple act of respect, to our neighbors, family, Spirit and ourselves. For extending genuine respect to others it shows the highest form of love, an unconditional love. So many people have given up their very lives to protect the freedoms that many take for granted. No matter where you are from we are all in this together. So respecting others for who they are and knowing that we are all divine beings created in the image and after the likeness of God is truly what a happy independence day is all about.

JULY 5th

A Step Closer To Moving Past Your Fear

When we act as the observer, or simply listen to a friend that is sharing with us their deepest feelings and sometimes struggles, it is easy to identify what may be a simple solution. But often it is not so simple for them; for they may already know what they should or could do to fix something they simply are afraid to do anything. They feel like they have no choice. The reality is that they are choosing to make no choice. Often time's people will be so afraid of the outcome that they avoid it all together. Rather than trusting that the outcome will go as it should, regardless of the uncomfortable steps it may take along the way. Just step up, move forward and know that every step is one closer to moving past your fear.

JULY 6th

Do What Your Designed To Do

What is it that keeps us from doing the things that we are designed to do? Most often we will list a whole bunch of reasons why we are not doing something. We are too busy, it is too challenging, it takes too long, we are not sure how to do it…. Stop for a second and listen to what you are telling others. We are expecting them to believe that all these reasons you've just given them is why we have been putting things off. Is it any wonder that we don't get the response from others that we may be hoping for? For with each reason we are searching for some validation that will justify why we are doing everything else but what it is we should be doing. So examine the roadblocks that are being presented and rather than stop completely, realize you have many options. Simply choose one.

JULY 7th

No Need To Defend

Feeling the need to defend our actions can be a very valuable indication that perhaps it is time to reevaluate the part that we may be playing in a certain situation. While one may feel justified in explaining their point of view it often is a futile attempt because the other person may choose not to see past their own idea. When you are able to simply give up being right and remember that perhaps there is a larger lesson at work and in the big scheme of things, everything will go, as it should. You can rest assured that if your actions and deeds were a result of pure intentions then you can take comfort in knowing that all you can ever do is simply your best and there is never a need to defend that.

JULY 8th

See Things As They Are

In times of frustration about wanting things to go a certain way we get lost in the ability to separate the line between optimistic and border line delusion. One of the biggest challenges we have is letting go of our preconceived ideas of how we wish something could be and be mindful to see things as they are. Our internal voice sometimes speaks to us in ways that we know in our heart to be true, but when the outside circumstances are not lining up to match what we are feeling, we often get deflated. And rather than continue forward in the certain optimistic fashion, we allow disappointment to push us right back into old safe patterns, patterns that we have tried so hard to move past. Be grateful that you can identify when you are in this place for that is the first step to moving further in the direction that you should go.

JULY 9th

Start By Changing How You Look At You

The hurt, shame and guilt that we feel about our past mistakes can often debilitate our progress. We become angry with our self and we lash out at everyone. Our constant punishment of our self often misleads us to feel like the universe is simply against us. Allowing yourself to feel what is going on inside you is the first step to healing. Give yourself the love and trust that others may have been withholding from you. If you stop to notice you will see that maybe they never held anything from us. Perhaps we wouldn't let them love us because we were unable and unwilling to love our self. While our past mistakes may need some attention it is important to change how we look at things starting with our self.

July 10th

Simply Because You Are You

Something magical happens when you take yourself out of your day-to-day environment and slow down. You stop worrying about all the things that seem to consume all your time and energy. Time itself seems to slow down and you feel like you can actually keep up. Having the opportunity to go somewhere where you are not responsible for anything more than just showing up and going with the flow feels amazing. Spending time with your true self and not the image you put on for the world, helps you remember how simple things can be. We often make things complicated and busy so we feel important and before you know it we are so overwhelmed. Slow down and find peace with the reality that you are important simply because you are you.

JULY 11th

Attachment And Connection

Attachment and connection are very different and while the words we choose to use may imply we are feeling one way, to another it is important to know the difference. Attachment infers that one is blurring the lines to the boundaries that may have been agreed upon by both parties. While connection simply is the state of which our souls are relating to another. If we are clear within our self on the intensity of the connection we have with another while remaining detached to some point we will be able to experience the genuine feelings that are contained within the lesson. For fear on ones part of being out of control may lead one to misinterpret words that are said to imply one is unclear. Trust Spirit to guide you with clarity through the experience and remind others while you may be genuine you are open and understand the circumstances.

JULY 12th

Who we are

We strive in our lives to be the person God created us to be. Most of the time we are not even sure who that is. The false beliefs we have about God are often reflected to the world in the person we appear to be. We wander around taking on the form and actions of a being we think everyone else will love and approve of. We act like one person at our job, another person to our family and another person to a stranger. We wonder who is this person we have become, why are we stuck and unhappy with behaving in a way that really doesn't reflect the real us? Then we notice we don't even really know who we are. As we develop a love and understanding about God it is then that we find our true self and become the genuine person we were created to be.

JULY 13th

Passion To Create

When you are very passionate about something it is very easy to excel at whatever you put your mind to. The people around you can see that what you are creating is an outlet into the world of a gift given to you by Spirit. Waking up every day and bringing your gifts to the world thru your service to others is what Spirit calls each of us to do. For when we feel unhappy and disconnected it is time to notice that perhaps we have completed another chapter in our journey. Lovingly bless the part you have played and return to that space that allows your passion to grow. For if you lose your passion for life, then you also lose a big portion of yourself.

JULY 14th

Feel Comfort In The Unknown

Rather than get caught up in your own fear of how you interpret what another may be feeling about how you are connecting with them, it is important for all involved to trust that feeling of knowing that you have with them. Enjoy that comfort in knowing and trusting that Spirit is at work and that each person is getting the lessons and teaching that are needed in the development of the journey. Fear of the expectations of another will take away from the beauty of what the connection is all about. Allow yourself to feel comfort in the unknown and know that all will unfold in the divine timing of exactly what you need and you will be able to remain centered as you open your heart to trust.

JULY 15th

Remain Centered

It can be a challenge at times to remain centered. Situations and circumstances happen in your day-to-day life and for a moment you let your emotions and fear get the best of you. You start to think that if you do a certain thing or behave a certain way then the outcome you didn't even realize you were hoping for would just happen. You become disappointed when things take a different turn all the while you knew that things will go, as they should. It is important to set yourself gently back on to your center, because things are going exactly how they should, so refocus, re-center and realize that what you are experiencing is just another baby step on to something that will be more amazing than you had even hoped for.

JULY 16th

Choosing To Walk Through Our Lesson

Spirit is around us in so many ways. We often get caught up in the business of our daily life. We get lost in our thoughts, our memories and sometimes our dreams. Many times we will be presented with a challenge we are to face. We lose sight of the blessing that is contained within the circumstances we'd rather run from. Finally we choose to walk through our lesson. While often they are painful, we must simply detach from that pain and look for the love. It is not always easy to see but if you look back on your life you will see that you have been learning to do this all along. In fact that is what we have all come here to do. See the love and know that it is everywhere present.

JULY 17th

Healing With Every Breath

When we slow down in our life long enough to notice all the healing that takes place in every moment, it can be quite an amazing realization. We spend so much time reacting to situations or simply going through the motions as we move on to something else. In our mind we think that we will fix or change our self later. We feel like our broken parts can be dealt with at another time. We sometimes even fool our self into thinking we are less or more broken then we appear to be. When we finally stop analyzing our self and surrender, we realize that miraculous healing has been going on all along. For if we are breathing, we are indeed healing with every single breathe. Taking in new and releasing the old.

JULY 18th

Spirit Working In You As You

Our body is such an amazing creation. Often times we misunderstand our own bodies because we don't know how to lovingly communicate with them. It is very much the same with people and relationships. While people have the ability to speak to us with words and actions, it really is not easier. The person speaking may or may not choose the words that express what they feel and we may not hear them in the ways they were intended, or perhaps we just don't get it. The body operates on such an advanced spiritual level that it does not need words, nor do we need ears to hear and feel what is being communicated. What we need to understand, is love, the things you have going on in your relationships with your body and even your loved ones can all be understood with the love of Spirit working in you as you.

JULY 19th

What Spirit Designed Friendship To Be

Allowing your loved ones to share how they truly feel about things helps you see who you really are. When you accept that others are entitled to feel what they feel, do what they do and you give them the space and freedom to express it to you, then you have truly understood what Spirit has designed friendship to be. Often times people over step their place by projecting their ideas and feelings on to the ones closest to them. They place unexpected boundaries and agendas on to the person by extending conditional love. In the end everyone gets hurt because when you are trying to measure up to the expectations of others not only have you lost the meaning of a true friend but you have lost sight of who you truly are.

JULY 20th

More In Store For You

It can be disappointing when something you have planned for doesn't work out. It is in these times that it is very important to understand that all things are as they should be. The dream job you think you wanted, the new relationship you've been dreaming of, or the letting go of something you have out grown are all indications that perhaps you have once again settled for much less then what Spirit has in mind for you. We tend to feel undeserving of some of the things we want most. In these cases we actually push them away. And while we may think we have things figured out it becomes more clear by the day that the only way to truly be happy is to trust that Spirit will always remind you that more is in store for you than you could ever dream of.

JULY 21st

Innocence Of A Baby

The most amazing reflection of Spirits love for us often comes in the form of a newborn baby. A gentle little person who has brought us the biggest reminder of what love really is. For such as the newborn who is so innocent that they radiate to all around them what pure Sprit looks like. How can one lay eyes on a baby and not feel love? Things are really simple; when you care for them they are content. They cry out when they are hungry, or when they need to be changed. Is it not that way for us to? The only difference is that for us the world does not look upon us as they do a baby. They forget to see our innocence just as we lose sight of our own. But we are all still that beautiful being in the eyes of Spirit.

JULY 22nd

Remembering Who We Are

It has been said by some that we are the sum total of our experiences. That the things we have been thru help mold us into the person we have become. Have you ever really thought about that? The soul of a person is eternal and has had many amazing experiences. While some experiences stay in our memory many of them slip away into a place we don't often recall. Perhaps a dream, a smell, a song or another person will remind us of a little part of our self that we have forgotten. Maybe we will remember a little bit more of who we are if we open our heart and our eyes to Spirit, not only will we remember who we really are but we will also remember each other. We will recall that we are nothing less than amazing.

JULY 23rd

Unexpected Moments Of The Unknown

It is often in the times that we are most ourselves when we can truly see others. The innocent opportunity to do the next right thing turns into an opportunity to have an experience you never saw coming. In the complete freedom of the moment you feel a connection that cannot be denied yet words are not available to begin to put an explanation together of what might be going on. You know in your heart that whatever comes next will be as it should be. Many times we get caught up in fear or the tangled webs of the human mind. All the while we know that we are safe to have a new exciting experience. If we can get past our own limited ideas of what we think we know then we can truly enjoy what Spirit has brought to us in the unexpected moments of the unknown.

JULY 24th

Contagious Positive Attitude

It remains a challenge at times to stay positive when everything around you seems to go differently than maybe you had hoped or expected. To compound your frustrations people close to you seem to think they know what is best for you. They start in with all the things they think you should do as well as pointing out all the things you should have done differently. Oh yea and don't forget, take note that they expect you will have the same experiences that have been frustrating them as well. They say it is out of concern for you that they are pointing all this out. That is when you draw in a large breath and smile and as you exhale you send them your love. Remember that a positive attitude can be just as contagious.

JULY 25th

Something Is Missed

It can often be shocking to see someone you know or think
you know behave in a manner that is less than graceful.
We all have views and perceptions about the people that
we have around us. We see things in different ways.
Sometimes we believe that people view us the same way
we view our self. Only later to learn that we have been
misjudged, misunderstood or misinterpreted. In any case
something is missed. Maybe we don't have all the details,
or perhaps we are so set on our own ideas that we have left
little or no room to notice that what is missing is the
realization that all is as it should be. And what we view as
a less than graceful behavior can actually be a very
important lesson for us all.

JULY 26th

Believe In Yourself

When someone believes in you, it is amazing how much more confident that we feel about ourselves. We are almost more willing than we normally would be to step outside our usual behaviors. We don't seem so scared to try something new. We are less likely to be concerned about failing. For when someone else believes in us we seem more willing to believe in our self. One part of us doesn't want to let them down and the other part has the courage to be daring, to take risks. Spirit reminds us how to believe in our self. How can we believe in those around us when we are unwilling to treat our self in the highest regard? Be willing to extend your love to others as they have done for you.

July 27th

Assumptions

Many times people make assumptions about you based on some perception that they may believe is true about you. It could be based on something you say or do. It could even be based on how you look or whom you are with. While many things are often not as they seem to be, it can be interesting when all parties make the realization that perhaps some assuming is going on. The key to unraveling an assumption before it starts is to ask questions. Most importantly you should genuinely listen for the answer, not just a validation to what you think you already know. For you might be pleasantly surprised by the things you may learn about someone when you create that space for things to just be. Just as others would be amazed what they would learn about you.

JULY 28th

Truth In Your Perfection

The biggest gift you can give to another is to respect that they are a perfect individual just as they are. It can be very evident that they don't feel even the least bit perfect. In fact they may be the first to point out a whole list of things they believe are wrong with them. While it is not our place to judge another there may very well be some actions and behaviors that support the things they are saying to be accurate. If someone believes something about themselves then they have made it their truth. While we may not be able to change their mind we can however continue to show them all the many perfect things that we see. It may take time, but at some point our friend may realize that perhaps our belief in their perfection will help them see it as not only our truth but theirs.

JULY 29th

What Is Your Body Telling You?

Most of us are aware that a physical symptom is often a result of a way of thinking or being. What are the things your body is telling you? And what are the actions you need to take? What we dismiss as one thing may be the subtle signs of something completely different. While it may not always be so severe that we need to seek help, it should defiantly not be dismissed as nothing. Maybe it should be an opportunity to search further. Perhaps the experience you will have includes others that you may meet along the way in places you would never normally go. Changing the physical behaviors that may be causing the problem will be the simple part. Changing the thinking will take the trusting of Spirit. So know that all is as it should be.

JULY 30th

Take A Baby Step

It can be very comforting to acknowledge and honor yourself for realizing that you have grown and survived some lessons that you never thought you could. When we experience a tragic event it can often affect us so deeply that we almost convince our self that this is the moment that will finally break us beyond repair. As we feel our entire world shattering around us it can often feel impossible to remember what grace feels like. The pain can be so unbearable that we don't even care to search for the strength to try. We finally surrender to the realization that we have actually hit rock bottom. We can lay down here and grovel or we can discover that the next logical step will finally be the first step towards the top. Even the longest journey begins with just a baby step.

JULY 31st

Wear A Furry Hat

Have you ever thought that you might like to hop on one foot to where you are going? While the world may expect us to walk in the usual normal way, maybe we would find it more fun and exciting to hop. Maybe we'd like to skip along the way. Maybe it may even be fun to wear silly clothes and a really furry hat while jumping rope to our destination. The important thing to realize is that we must make the time to do the things in a way that makes us feel happy and excited. When we choose to do everything in the ways that others feel is best for us, it can often leave us feeling limited and unfulfilled. While we may not want to jump rope to work it is nice to know we have the choice. Be brave enough to do things in your own creative way.

AUGUST 1st

In Your Haste

As you busy yourself in day-to-day activities sometimes things will be overlooked. Your intention may be to get to it later, or perhaps you just blow it off completely. Other times you may not even realize that you have missed something. It may not be noticed until a hurt friend finally finds a voice and decides to speak up. Then something that seemed so simple becomes a little more complicated. Then you realize in all your haste of things that don't really matter, you speed past small things that would truly make a difference in a really big way. So while you may think it is the other person you have hurt, you may notice that the person who is hurting the most is you.

AUGUST 2nd

Spirit Dwells In You

In the circle of life it can often be a challenge when you are moving from one situation to another. A loved one completes their journey here and then returns to Spirit and the people left behind sift slowly thru this new experience. While on one hand you celebrate a life well lived and find comfort in knowing they have gone home, the other hand is desperately trying to hold your heart together. You're grasping in all directions in an attempt to pull yourself together, searching for the comfort that will calm your very soul. You close your eyes and take a deep breath and suddenly you remember that what you are searching for is right inside of you. The love of Spirit dwells in your very being. This is the comfort we all share.

A UGUST 3rd

Make A New Choice

So what are the things that keep reappearing in your life? What pattern seems to repeat itself over and over but with new details and a different face? It's a little bit similar to the last time but somehow you convince yourself that this time is different. You examine the details and attempt to analyze what may be going on. As you examine this lesson that is simply a more creative version of the same old lesson you've been through many times, you finally understand that unless you change your perception and open your mind and heart enough to notice, that until you gently take the time to walk through this and heal, it will simply return again and again, patiently waiting for you to make a new choice.

AUGUST 4th

See Things As They Are

Learning to accept things simply as they are can often be the biggest challenge that a person can face. On one hand we assign a meaning to something that may or may not even be close to what is implied or intended by another. We often read more into something by creatively thinking that a situation or action of another is centered around us. We get all caught up in the illusion that our perception is the truth of the matter. But whose truth is it? And honestly we spend a lot of energy making something bigger than it really is. For every time we interpret something and add our own meaning to it, we lose sight of what Spirit has presented to us because we choose to see it from our limited view. Expand your sight to see it for what it is.

AUGUST 5th

The Space To Learn

Sometimes a person may over step their place in a loved one's life when they think they know what is best for them. Most of the time we spend trying to figure out the things that are in our highest good. While we often miss the mark, one thing is certain, valuable lessons were presented. If we take the time to examine our own lives we may realize that we are of no authority to decide for others what we have been unable to do for our self. True unconditional love shows respect and gives you the space and support to make your own choices, the true test is that you will also show support and respect for other when things do not go as planned. We each deserve the space to learn as we go.

A UGUST 6th

Getting Things Done

Things in our daily life can seem so hectic that we don't know which way we are going. We go from one task to another frantically trying to complete them all. We start one thing, than add a few more and attempt to juggle them all. We put a small amount of attention into many places spreading our self so thin that we are unable to be as present as we should to effectively get a single thing done. Who said all these things had to be done right this second? Who said that they had to be done in a particular way? Who is that person that is smothering you about why you can't do more? Take a moment to go within and find your center, recharge your soul and allow Spirit to show you a peaceful way to get things done.

A UGUST 7th

Answer The Cries

People cry out to each other for love. These cries take on many forms. Some are subtle while others appear to be so obvious. Fighting and screaming at each other in a hope that they will be heard is so common. Back and forth go the hurtful words, the glaring eyes, the angry actions. When someone is hurting us in any form it is important to look beyond their actions and our perceptions and see the larger picture. They are hurting. So rather than react to another with the same sad behavior, you can choose to react in love. For when you extend love to a hurting heart it will soften. It will slowly begin to open and allow your love, the love of Spirit to enter to answer the cries.

AUGUST 8th

Embrace Of Grace

As the experiences of our lives unfold, perhaps you can
find words to describe them. Many times the feelings we
have are too intense for words. We feel the song of grace
and joy traveling through our body. We may also feel
deep pain and sadness. While we may struggle to find a
word, a thought or even an action to share with another
how we are feeling, we often are unable to even make
sense of it within our self. The five senses of our physical
body may not begin to explain just what may be going on.
Close your eyes, take a deep breath and simply experience
for yourself what Spirit may be saying to you. In this
moment you will feel the embrace of grace.

AUGUST 9th

Within Us

The way a person feels about themselves is often how they feel about others. When we are angry with our self we can easily see things in other people that create that same feeling. So what are the feelings you are having of yourself? When we realize that everything we will ever need or want from any person or situation starts within our self. It becomes much easier to live the life we have been wanting. When we search for happiness and security outside or our self it becomes not only impossible to find but even more impossible to maintain. When you finally start to understand how amazing you truly are then others will start to see it too.

AUGUST 10th

Love Is Who We Are

When the people in our lives that we truly love move on, it can often leave us feeling hurt and lost. We may see this in a negative way at first but as we start to review all the ways they may have made a difference in our life we will discover that they are still very much with us. Sometimes it may even feel like they are more a part of us then when they were still with us. The love we have with another has no beginning and no end. It is the very essence of who we are. Spirit sends us examples of how we are loved in the form of other people. When we are able to see the love in all situations despite how we might have labeled them we will be able to see that love is who we are.

A UGUST 11th

Worth It Everytime

Making a decision in your life to take the steps that will lead you to your dreams can often bring up fear. Fear of not being good enough, fear of failure, fear of giving up something for something that isn't mapped out. Think back in your life at the other times you have made decisions. The fear was far outweighed by the joy of living the life that makes you happy. It may not have always been easy but it was defiantly always worth it. And it will be worth it this time too! In fact it will be worth it every time. So take the next step into the direction of your dreams and you will remember how it really feels to be living your dreams. You are defiantly good enough so don't give up.

AUGUST 12th

Power Of Words

The power of words has a tremendous impact in our daily lives. While one person believes they are speaking clearly, what may be heard or perceived may be completely different from what that person was actually trying to say. The spoken word often travels through a very complex filter system. A thought originates in the mind and as a person prepares to say it, it has bounced around changing in unique ways before it is set free into the world. Once it is out there, it can be received or perceived in many ways. Be clear with your words and thoughts for once they are shared it is quite possible to heal or harm, either another or one's self.

A UGUST 13th

Next Stage Of Growth

When we transition from one experience to another it can bring up many emotions, not only in our self but in those around us. A transition is the first step into the change we need in our life to experience our next stage of growth. When we finish and complete a certain experience it becomes necessary to move on to the next opportunity. Choosing how we react can bring us into a state of bliss or torment. Once we accept and realize that it is all part of our unending journey it becomes clear that in every moment Spirit has brought us a new beginning.

AUGUST 14th

Supporting Others

When we choose to support another in some way, we may think we are doing something that is in their highest good. This may be in fact true. Stop for a moment and you will realize that it is also for your highest good. When the people of our communities support each other, it becomes quite obvious that when we work together honoring and respecting those around us, we can achieve amazing things. Many people are searching for peace, while all the time it is right there in front of them. Reach out from your center to support others and you will also be honoring and supporting yourself.

AUGUST 15th

Profound Love

When you experience a true and profound unconditional love you begin to understand that is how Spirit loves us. It is constant and never ending. The circumstances in our lives will be constantly changing and while we may sometimes feel a separation, not only from Spirit but our self and everyone around us, it will take only a still quiet moment to remember and feel that we are truly loved and how it feels to love others in that way. When the people in your life move on it is then that you will truly understand that the profound love is still there and very present in your life, and so are they.

AUGUST 16th

The Gift Of Your True Self

As you begin to truly know who you really are, you will also be able to communicate with others in a whole new way. The clarity in the words you speak will be a reflection of how you truly feel and others will be able to relate to you in new ways. The gift of your true self to others is the biggest blessing you can bring to this lifetime. Many times when we live our life form this way of being it makes a profound impact on other people we meet along our journey. People are drawn to those that are taking the steps to know themselves truly, for they can see you are willing to take the steps to also know them.

August 17th

Who We Really Are Created To Be

You will feel the pull of becoming all that you were created to be. As we wake up each day we are offered many experiences that are all preparing us towards this goal. When we think we achieve this, it is then that we realize we are able to be more. The depths at which we grow do not even come close to the vastness at which we can become more of who we really are created to be. We are made in the image and after the likeness of God. Listen to the winds, look up to the stars and you will see just a tiny piece of how magnificent and boundless that God is. You will also see that this is how you were created.

A UGUST 18th

Look At Our Beliefs

When we begin to take the steps to learning who we are, we also start taking the steps to unlearn most of what we have been taught. We begin to question why we believe the things we believe, we start to unravel all the rules we have lived our life by. Whether we consciously choose to break down the beliefs in our life or situations and experiences cause us to feel challenged by them, we will be able to notice that most of what we have been taught is simply not true for us anymore. At some point it may have been, but as all things change so does the need for us to look once again at our beliefs. For beliefs create our behavior and that changes everything.

AUGUST 19th

Drops In The Ocean

There is often a fine line between understanding we are all on our own journey and realizing we are all one and on the same journey. While our experiences and pathways will be unique and different the end result is exactly the same. We have come to this experience of life to remember who we truly are. And that is we are one with God, one with each other. We often fight for our separateness, validation from others that we are special and important. While we all have profound value we are but drops in the same ocean. Without each and everyone it would not be as magnificent as it truly is.

AUGUST 20th

Be That Love To Others

The innocence and purity that is present in a newborn baby is also very much a part of us. The world respects and understands that a little baby comes here pure and in need of our love and nurturing as it begins to grow. A baby did not come here with rigid boundaries and beliefs; they simply love others as they were created. When we care for those around us in ways less than loving or from a place of fear we are teaching them how we our self want to be treated. We all really want to be loved and nurtured in a pure way but often that is not the case. Always remember that you truly are loved by Spirit in just that way. Be that love to others.

A UGUST 21st

Identify Your Stuff

Being able to acknowledge in your relationships what may be your stuff to work on and what may be another's is the most productive tool you have to work with. When someone pushes your button by what they may say or do it is your responsibility to look at why you may be feeling the way you are feeling. On some level you are not at a peaceful place within yourself because if you were, there wouldn't be that reaction. If you can identify what is really going on inside yourself you will see that these experiences are the perfect opportunities to heal those places that we may think we have moved past. The same is true when it appears you have pushed their button.

AUGUST 22nd

The Call To Grow

Many times it is easy to hide from the painful things you need to heal by putting more energy into things that can distract you from doing the work that at some point must be done. We become the best at our job, we become the pillar of respect in our community, we may even become the worst alcoholic or drug addict, any case it is exactly the same. We put all our attention into something else that will help us hide, something that may dull or numb the pain, something that will keep us so busy that we can't slow down long enough to hear Spirit calling us to grow. We are so afraid of the pain that we forget that something good comes from everything. Be open to know that all is as it should be and you will see the good. Don't be afraid to do the work.

A UGUST 23rd

Say What You Need To Say

When we lose track or become distant from another it may feel impossible to find forgiveness and healing. We really believe that perhaps the situation may never be fixed and that it will always be this way. We may carry a lot of guilt around the things we have done and how it may have affected those around us. Things happen exactly as they must in the big scheme of things or else it would have happened differently. So look at these relationships and how they appear to be fractured and then allow that divine part of yourself to emerge and go forward in a genuine and loving way. Say what you need to say simply because you need to say it. They may not hear or accept it, but the miracle has happened because you have finally done your part. And that is all you can do.

AUGUST 24th

Roots Of A Friendship

Often the roots of a friendship may run very deep. The history may cover the span of many years. It is wise to notice that it is still really in its very beginning stages that it has infinite possibilities of where it might go. For as deep as the roots may appear to go there are many undiscovered and amazing experiences yet to be had, once you remove the limits and labels that you may have placed on the relationship based on the beliefs or ideas that you may have though the friendship was serving. As you continue to learn more about yourself you will realize that you are just beginning to know others as well.

AUGUST 25th

Victim Or Victorious

The circumstances and situations in our life sometimes give us the false appearance that leads us to believe we do not have a choice in the situation. Interestingly enough we are simply choosing not to make a choice. The freedom one finds in their own life is to realize and understand that the one sure thing you do have is the power of choice. Now whether you exercise that power or not is the ultimate choice you can make. It is the difference in being a victim or becoming victorious. While these decisions and choices you may be faced with may not be easy, take great comfort in knowing that in the end you always have a choice.

AUGUST 26th

Truly Listen

Have you ever noticed that when someone says "hey I need to talk to you about something" we automatically think the worst? We start analyzing what we may have done to upset them. We start thinking up all the reasons and justifications we have for doing the things we may or may not have done. The time arrives where we sit down to have this talk. Never noticing that we may be so caught up in our own ideas of what is going to be said and how we will respond that we never truly listen to what they may be trying to say. What we are hearing has gone through this crazy filter that we use to try and fit it into alignment with our thoughts. Never thinking once that what they want to say may be positive. Let them speak while you truly listen.

AUGUST 27th

Higher Regard

The people that are closest to us seem to take most of the disrespect we can possibly dish out. Of course they don't take on the heaping amount we put on our self but nonetheless they bear the brunt that comes along with this crazy assumption that we are entitled to act this way. Many times we give a complete stranger more respect than we give to our self and our family. While we think we are being respectful it shows in the experiences we are having with them that maybe we should make a better effort to treat them in a higher regard rather than let our past history determine the way we will treat them. We can only hope they will do the same.

AUGUST 28th

Let Your Defenses Down

It can be interesting how in one experience it can be the most amazing and beautiful situation and when you move into the next situation all these feelings and things come up that you felt like you had dealt with. When we truly let our defenses down and allow our self to feel what is going on around us it can be a little uncomfortable to feel so vulnerable. We may realize that we have been trying to convince our self that we feel one way about something when we truly feel differently. Take a moment to look at your life and all of the many beautiful aspects and you will be able to see that you truly have grown and all is as it should be.

AUGUST 29th

Trust God First

As we look to Spirit for guidance we also seek ways to justify why we choose not to listen. We pray for God to bring us that opportunity to find love and when the pieces line up and fall into place our fear steps up in front and demands our attention. What if you know what's best for you? What if you think it is simply easy to feel nothing rather than take the risk of being hurt? It seems silly when you think about it, how could we possibly know more than God does about what is best for us? When all the times we chose to do things without him often resulted in everything but love. While the hurt we bring upon our self helps us grow and become closer to God, all he asks is that we trust him first and perhaps we will finally feel the love.

AUGUST 30th

Your True Beauty

When your insecurities raise their ugly little heads it's time to take a step back and see where it was you decided to behave separately from your connection to Spirit again. Allowing your weakness to take over the powerful being you are in your true form only brings you chaos. The ego is once again present to fight for its very existence. All those feelings of never being good enough, pretty enough or truly loved and wanted simply just another reflection of how you were feeling about yourself. So what if another person doesn't think you are enough. Ask yourself enough for what? Enough for someone who doesn't see your true beauty? Don't let them take away your ability to see it. For they have not even seen their own worth.

AUGUST 31st

Special Milestone In The Journey

Certain dates have specific meanings for everyone. Perhaps it is a birthday, anniversary of an occasion or a holiday. In any case each and every day has great significance in our overall journey. Some days are huge milestones and reminders of how we have grown. We will one day understand the value of the average every ordinary day that we often don't reflect on or perhaps even see its value until another experience marks a day that changes our lives. We sometimes take for granted that this day was someone's big day in some way for maybe many years. And then one day they are gone and it remains in our heart another special milestone in the journey we shared with them.

SEPTEMBER 1st

Finding True Peace

Sitting outside, disconnected from your phone, your job and your daily routine can be the best way to connect with what is really important. Listening to the silence can speak louder to your soul than the hundreds of voices shouting at you constantly. Listen to the sounds of nature, the wind blowing, the birds singing, the leaves rustling in the wind, it's as if you can hear all of your loved ones feelings, the ones they don't say. The connection to Spirit and all that is can be heard in the quite of your mind. Allowing your true nature to take the front seat in this day will help you keep yourself on your path of finding true peace and happiness, as you trust Spirit to guide you.

SEPTEMBER 2nd

The Bigger Picture

In your moment of doubt, lift your head high and you will see the support that Spirit has sent all around you. Perhaps it is a hawk that flies overhead to remind you to see the up above perspective to something. Maybe it is in the smile of a longtime friend. It may simply be one look in the mirror to remind you that you are the one you have been waiting for. Whatever fears and doubts you may be facing is simply only one small piece of a bigger picture that is at work here. Focus on the other pieces and perhaps the doubts and fears won't seem so big. The beauty of the overall picture is sure to catch your eye and remind you of what you truly need to focus on.

SEPTEMBER 3rd

Choose To Climb

Breaking down walls can be very difficult. Sometimes it may even feel impossible. When we connect with someone that we care about it can often times add reinforcement to these walls. The fact that they are present is the first step to removing that simple first brick. While we may remove a couple it seems like we add a few new ones. We truly fear that we will never be able to remove enough bricks to let someone in and that no one will be willing to climb. Remember that Spirit will hold your hand as you walk thru this process and he will be there to guide you as you choose to climb the wall of the people you love. For choosing to climb you will learn how to truly love yourself.

SEPTEMBER 4th

Supporting Another

Sometimes it's hard to remember that things we think are our business really aren't. We wonder how we really fit into another person's life. We believe that because they don't share certain things with us that they don't care about us. We feel like in the silence of unsaid things that they are being dishonest. But really what is going on is that they are going thru their own journey and we are but a supporting actor in their story, just as they are for us. We too have things we don't share but it doesn't lessen the connection that is shared, it simply gives us the opportunity to really get to what we need to work on in our self.

SEPTEMBER 5th

The Gift Of Our Experience

When we try to define the role that we play in another person's life we often make our self feel crazy. As the areas we need to work on in our life come presenting themselves we often lose sight of what is truly going on. The divine nature can be revealed if we simply step back and allow the pieces to fall into place. No matter our efforts we cannot force the pieces into place any faster than they are supposed to be there. Patience is to be revered for without it we will simply self-destruct a beautiful experience before it is time. Leaving our past hurts and regrets behind with the love of forgiveness of Spirit will help us to move forward with an open heart to receive the gift of our experience with another.

SEPTEMBER 6th

Trust Spirit To Work In Your Life

We hide our true self for fear of being rejected or made fun of. We pretend to be something we are not in hopes of pleasing others. Sometimes we hide our self so deeply that we are not even sure of who we are. If you are truly willing to trust Spirit to work in your life, you will realize that you have never known yourself. You have hidden yet another delusion of who you think you are because if we all truly understood who it is each of us have come here to be there is no way we would be able to hide it. Being made in and after the image of God is who we are said to be. When we realize this divine connection you will find that the more you learn to love yourself the more connected you will feel to Spirit.

SEPTEMBER 7th

Closer To The Heart Of God

When someone we love is taken home to be with God we cry for missing what we had. We miss being able to pick up the phone and call them, embrace them in a hug. Our heart aches for feeling left behind. For the unsaid things, the undone actions, just knowing they were there for us. As we experience the many levels of grief we start to uncover all the beautiful moments that our loved ones brought to our life, we start to feel grateful for all the time that we did have with them and how they truly touched our hearts. As we draw closer to the heart of God in our times of weakness we realize that they have never left us, they are as close to us as the beating of our heart and still supporting us as we continue on our journey.

SEPTEMBER 8th

The Bliss We All Long For

I have heard it said that ignorance is bliss. When we don't know things we are often more receptive, willing to put our self out there to have the experience be at its best. Our so-called ignorance is a tool that quite possibly gets us out of our own way. When we stop thinking a situation completely through while we add hundreds of different outcomes and scenarios, we will stop exhausting our self mentally before anything has even begun. The unknown and the willingness to let it unfold, as it will, create the bliss that we all long for. Maybe we should rethink our definition of ignorance. The beauty is found in all the things that we don't know that we don't know.

SEPTEMBER 9th

The Ego Wants To Play

When the urge to close down on another person comes out because you feel hurt, remember that it's really yourself you are about to close down on. You spend your energy going thru conversations you want to have with them or making up conversations you think they may be planning to have with you. All the while your ego is trying to fight for exactly what you should do and say so that you will not look like an idiot. The ego wants answers and reasons to every little detail and it can't stand that perhaps you are being played. But are you really being played? Stand up and be determined to trust Spirit in this instance, for many instances will be like this one. Realize that your ego is the one that wants to play.

S EPTEMBER 10th

Your Childhood Friend

Reconnecting to a friend from childhood has the wonderful ability to remind you of many parts of yourself that you have long since forgotten. Life times have passed since you last saw them. Many things have changed for both of you, but what remains the same is the close innocence that you shared before you went out into the world and began to get hurt. You notice when you look at your friend it is so easy to see that innocent child that you had grown to love so much. You trusted them completely because you knew nothing different. It reminds you that we are not our circumstances, nor are we unworthy of love or even unable to love. We look at our friend and we truly understand the meaning of unconditional love. If you're able to love them past their hurts then you will also be able to love yourself as God loves you.

SEPTEMBER 11th

The Greatest Tragedy

Often in great tragedy we are reminded of what is really important. We step above our own small needs to realize that we are all in this journey together. When our brother is hurting, we too are hurting. When we feel alone in our struggles a great tragedy that often shakes us up enough to take the time to work with others in helping those around us begin to recover.   We love others in the hopes that they will recover from the tragic events in their life. In this process we are able to open our heart enough to start trusting others to reach out to us as well.   The greatest tragedy of all is when we choose to struggle alone and not allow our self to be connected to the love of others.

SEPTEMBER 12th

A Major Turning Point

Learning to accept and even embrace our dark side will lead us closer to discovering how to finally allow our true light to shine. Many times we are stuck in our disappointment of how we are feeling when things seem to be going what appears to be terribly wrong. Who is to really say that anything can be labeled as right or wrong? What may be wrong to someone might be exactly what the other person needs to experience at that time in order to grow. The darkest times in our life are usually a major turning point that will remind us that we will get through anything if we are willing to take the time to see that every experience helps mold us into the person we are truly meant to be.

SEPTEMBER 13th

Acknowledge Your Hurt

How do you keep a positive disposition when your feelings are hurt? One could choose to lash out an speak up out of anger or you could simply breath in and remind yourself that it really isn't personal. Breathing in is the first step to maintaining your peace. Lashing out simply causes things to elevate and old wounds to resurface. You have to simply try to see the love that exists in the situation rather than choosing to see the negative things that are causing you to feel hurt. Acknowledge to yourself that you're hurt and then be honest enough with yourself and others that love you to try to see things from another perspective.

SEPTEMBER 14th

True Connection

Sometimes in the simplest of moments with our self or another we realize that our true connection requires no words at all. While we may have many things to say or perhaps ponder, the feeling that comes with a look or a smile says more to our heart than a thousand words. A simple hello or I love you can say it all. Finding the ability in yourself to appreciate and recognize these moments is one of the most profound gifts you can give yourself. For when one can truly honor another for who they are then every encounter will reflect back to us the magnificence of who Spirit truly created you to be.

SEPTEMBER 15th

Support Others

A lot can be said for and by the actions of a man. What would cause such behavior? Usually we don't have the opportunity to see all sides in a situation. Whether it is the beginning or the resolution each action plays a vital role in the overall experience. What appears to be one way may in fact be completely different. Choosing to honor and support others in their decisions whether we understand or not is the loving behavior that Spirit would have us demonstrate. In many situations we must stand for our own truth in a way that will not be popular with another. Be willing to honor and respect your feelings and it will be made clear the valuable lesson to be learned by all.

SEPTEMBER 16th

What Are You Giving Back?

People put self imposed ideas and limitations on them self and often believe that someone else has them stuck. They may defiantly be stuck. Freedom comes when we change our thinking, open our mind to new ideas and most importantly allow Spirit to move in and through us in our daily life. If you think someone should love you a certain way, they should talk to you a certain way or perhaps do things a particular way in order for you to feel loved, then it is time to look at yourself and notice what are you giving back? How are you treating yourself? Make a choice and stand strong in your decision but love others enough to do things the way they choose to.

SEPTEMBER 17th

A Brighter Today

A person may choose to use a drug, take a drink or hide behind a huge wall. In any of these cases it appears to be a cry for love. An attempt to bury some hurt; slow yourself down enough so that you can't think about anything at all. Who are they trying to hide from and what are they trying to bury? It doesn't matter because we are all doing the same thing, hiding from the same person. We are struggling with our self and all the guilt we refuse to let go of. What good is it doing us to continue to hold on to it? While you may not use a drug or even a drink, perhaps you work too much or move from one relationship to another. Let go and face your guilt and finally walk away and into a brighter today.

SEPTEMBER 18th

One Persons Ego

One person's ego may be so overwhelming that it is difficult to deal with them. So large in fact that you struggle to see past it and into the person they truly are. You may even have to fight the urge to prove them wrong. Being the bigger person in a situation that feels unfair can almost make you feel even worse. Our own ego fights to justify the rights and wrongs while hoping we will refuse to see the good in the other person. For in our way of thinking we don't want to look foolish to everyone else. While we can't be responsible for the actions brought on by the ego of another person we can take some pride and ownership in our own because that is all we are responsible for.

SEPTEMBER 19th

The Right Choice For You

When you make a choice be willing to endure all of the consequences and situation that may arise from it. Someone may choose to make you feel like you've made a poor choice, they may also want to punish you for doing things in your own way. Often times other people don't even realize that they are doing this. They are hurt and angry on some level and they decided to make you pay for how they are feeling, make you prove that your deserving of their respect for this second chance they are allowing. So take a moment to think things through and then decide for yourself if this is really the choice that is right for you.

SEPTEMBER 20th

Your Heart Wants What Spirit Is Offering

What is your heart saying to you right now? That feeling you have of knowing that everything will go as it should, will help you calm down the drama that wants to take over. Many times we know what we want in our heart but don't exhibit the love and or patience that will help us get to that point in our life. Stepping aside and allowing Spirit to work in our life will yield far greater results than you could ever imagine or dream of for yourself. We strive for one thing and then settle for less, far less than what Spirit has in mind. When you're willing to listen to your heart you will notice that it wants the very same things that Spirit is offering.

SEPTEMBER 21st

Love Without Limits

When you're willing to love someone else enough to be truly happy for them whether it will include you or not, then you have truly understood how God loves us. He gives us the free will and choice to do as we please whether or not it includes him. The wise person knows that everything includes him, especially the times you seem to exclude him. He is there loving and supporting us all the while. Waiting for us to remember that it is impossible for him to leave us, we are all one. It is just like that with our loved ones here in this journey. Though we may not physically travel together at some point they too are still as close to us as the beating of our heart. So don't be afraid to love without limits because true genuine love does not have limits.

SEPTEMBER 22nd

Trust Spirit Above All

Sometimes a situation may arise that challenges everything you may believe about how something may go. First the uncontrollable fear takes over and your mind races with all the ridiculous outcomes that will surely happen. Then you hear this voice that reminds you to have faith and remain diligent regardless of how things may look. What seems to appear obvious may go completely different. In any case it is important to remember that everything will go exactly as it should. A bigger lesson is at work. Although it may be clear later, just always remember that your faith will carry you through any situation. Trust Spirit above all.

SEPTEMBER 23rd

Everything Is A Reflection Of Spirit

Getting out into the world and taking time to notice all the things around you can remind you that everywhere you look it is possible to see what Spirit has created. Every rock, every mountain, every cloud, every cactus, every single thing that exists is a reflection of Spirit. When we over think things or add a label to it, it is then that we our self devalue the beauty in the simplest thing. For once we compare it to something else or think we really understand something based on our thinking or another's opinion or idea, we stop taking the time to receive the many gifts that come to us in the simplest form which is to just be. Everything is beautiful in the eyes of Spirit.

SEPTEMBER 24th

What You May Really Be Learning

While one may think they are in charge of all the details of a circumstance based on what their past experiences and feeling have been it is also important to realize that every situation is teaching you a valuable lesson on your journey. While you may discount or lessen the importance a person may play in your life based on the role you think they play, Spirit is ultimately showing you other things that will truly help you learn more about who you are. While our head struggles to be in charge and make sense of everything it is wise to realize what we think has very little to do with what we may really be learning.

SEPTEMBER 25th

Trust Spirit To Lead The Way

The outcome of a situation may take a very unexpected route in order to end up as it should go. People and situations may be stuck in such a place that it takes drastic measures and events to shift things into a different direction. If one behaves with proper principles and a strong sense of self confidence and integrity during an event that otherwise would anger or hurt you, it will be a lot easier to see that Spirit is at work in even this situation. Maybe the only way a person can walk away from a situation that they have become complacent in is to push them to a point of action. Know that some things don't need to be explained, trust Spirit to lead the way.

SEPTEMBER 26th

Clear Communication

So many feelings can be hurt when a person cannot be honest with themselves or the others around them. A situation with unclear boundaries and circumstances may arise and when one person questions the details, things can get out of balance quickly if the other party is unable or unwilling to take responsibility for their lack of clear communication. While one person may think they have been clear, the actions and the misunderstanding of another is an obvious indication that something is off track. It can be a challenge to see things clearly when your emotions have been charged. Take a step back and assess your part and know that Spirit will lead you if you let him.

S EPTEMBER 27th

Take Back Your Power

When one gives away their power to another it can set your entire world into a dramatic tailspin. It can be hard to identify what is making you so angry. Is it the other person's actions? Perhaps you are angry with yourself for allowing another person into a place that is vulnerable. We often extend our self too much to another in the hope that they will love us. We allow them to have much more control over how we feel. We are unable to see past our own illusions of what may be in our highest good because we have once again attached our self to an outcome. Take back your power and remember that you know what you need to do.

SEPTEMBER 28th

It Is Safe

A person may not realize just how much of their heart another person has. When a situation arises that you didn't see coming it can often open a wound you thought you had healed. Your mind begins to throw in thoughts that represent a past hurt or situation that started a pattern to how you may choose to react to things in the future. Before you have time to recognize what is going on you may have already lashed out in anger towards another. All this is in an attempt to protect yourself from getting hurt. When we feel vulnerable to another we often add bricks to the fortress we have built around our heart. Know that it is safe to let them in. Spirit is at work.

SEPTEMBER 29th

Choose To Stand

Believing in yourself enough to honor and respect the feelings you are having and the situations you are encountering will help you heal many of the wounds you have tried to ignore. It is very easy to walk away when things get difficult. The true strength of a person lies in the ability to stand strong in what you know is true when things get tough. To stay and fight against your own inner demons in order to find the peace and love in your circumstances takes great courage. To trust Spirit enough in all situations to see that you are safe and protected will give you more strength and courage then you ever realized you had. Choose to stand firmly instead of running.

SEPTEMBER 30th

Seeing From A Place Of Love

Why do we feel so hurt and rejected by a loved one when they say something that is hard for us to hear? Instead of noticing that they are just trying to speak up and be honest with us, we take it as a personal attack. All along it really has nothing to do with us, but perhaps a wound is being exposed in them based on the part we are playing. We can choose to dwell in the inauthentic feelings that we are having or we can try to see the situation from a place of love. What is causing us to take their words so personal that we allow our self to be pushed out of our healthy way of thinking? Perhaps in some way we identify with what they have said. Be open to hearing what is being said so that you may finally heal a wound that has once again returned.

OCTOBER 1st

What You Perceive As Lack

While you may think you are struggling in parts of your life, due to a lack of finances, job security or a many number of other things, really you are not. Perhaps it is time to revisit the simple side of life. Sitting outside in nature listening to all the many sounds around you can remind you that perhaps you are the one making things complicated in your life. The things that matter most in life don't require all the superficial circumstances that seem to present themselves in what you may perceive as lack. While one may need physical things to exist in this world, what one truly needs are all the things that can't be seen. The biggest gift is love.

OCTOBER 2nd

Brick By Brick

People spend a lot of time trying to protect themselves from being hurt. Brick by brick they build a wall of protection, a wall that is made up of dysfunctional ways of being. What is it that we are trying to protect ourselves from? The one person that really can cause us the most pain and damage in our life sits center stage in this grand, almost majestic fortress we have constructed. It can almost appear to be safe until you finally realize that it is not others you are keeping out but a prison you yourself have been locked into. The key holder and warden is you dressed in the misery and fear of your past. It is time to make a change and set yourself free.

OCTOBER 3rd

Time Well Spent

Being patient and trusting Spirit to guide you along your path can be a very slow and steadfast process. Learning patience and how to trust that things will unfold in a beautiful way can be a challenge. We want to run ahead carelessly without regard for safety. We think we know a faster way to get to where we think it is we want to go. In our haste we become sloppy and cut corners thinking we are saving time. The end result we arrive to on our own is then incomplete and often requires us to do it again differently. Trust that Spirit will guide you to be complete in your journey and in the long run it is all time well spent.

OCTOBER 4th

The Higher Call To Love

When you open your heart completely and allow Spirit to enter, you will discover an entirely new way of living your life. While you may have experienced some form of love before, partnering with Spirit will take you to the ultimate level of how love was intended to feel. You begin to experience a new relationship with yourself, and as you extend that love to those around you, it becomes effortless in how easy it is to expand your heart to depths you never realized were within you. The higher call to love is what helps us to grow. All you have to do to answer is open your heart.

OCTOBER 5th

The Warrior Within You

The fear a person carries around with them can often rob them of the many wonderful gifts that this life can bring. On our journey to self-discovery we can often hide behind fear in an attempt to avoid pain. If you look back over your life you will see that many of your painful experiences are what pushed you to the next level. Changing your way of thinking and embracing the idea that Spirit really does have your best interest in mind will allow you to walk through the scary parts knowing the whole time that you are safe and protected. Because within you Spirit has created a warrior who can endure all this life may bring.

OCTOBER 6th

The Fortress Of Your Heart

It is very easy to guard your heart so tightly that it becomes almost impossible to allow anything or anyone in enough to feel something. You become so desensitized that not only do you not feel love but most of the time you feel nothing at all. You believe you are smart because you no longer feel that aching pain. The subtle attempts that another may make to show you love may go completely unnoticed. They too have great fear and thick walls, so how can you each move on to more when you've become so hardened that any effort made feels impossible. Allow Spirit to enter the fortress of your heart so that you may finally see that it is safe to let other in as well.

OCTOBER 7th

The Love Of Those Around Us

One of the most loving things you can do when you are in a relationship with another is to honor and respect them just as they are. For when you think someone needs to be a certain way, have particular thoughts or opinions in order to gain your love or approval, you have just put conditions that will never be met. You have also become a hypocrite because deep down inside of yourself is the person who desires to be loved just as they are. Most of the time it takes our loved ones to help us realize who we are. For in our mistakes and shortcomings the love of those around us can often be the very thing that helps us learn to do things better the next time.

OCTOBER 8th

Honoring The Love

Many times when a relationship ends and people decide to go separate ways they take out their hurt on the other by simply adding more hurt. Fighting over material things or even things that were done or said often distract you both from what is really going on. If you choose to move on, then simply move on. Try to find a peaceful way to honor what it was that brought you together in the first place. Somewhere along the way the love was no longer honored. The pain built up enough to push you to the next step. So stop being angry at the other person and embrace the idea that something else is in store for you both. Walk away honoring the love of the past and of the new future.

OCTOBER 9th

It Never Has To End

The excitement of a new love can sometimes help you see the beauty all around you. It is also a new opportunity to practice trusting Spirit and yourself to accept the love you really deserve. Many times we feel like we don't really deserve something so good and we waste precious valuable time wondering when it will all end and we will go back to wishing for something more. Often times this way of thinking actually causes us to self-destruct something so beautiful because we constantly doubt that we really should live our life and be this happy. The real beauty comes in knowing that it never has to end and that is truly how Spirit created love to be, for we ourselves are love.

OCTOBER 10th

Beyond A Plan

When it seems complicated to make plans and organize your schedule, it may be time to notice that perhaps you are being called to stay flexible. You may think you know how things should go. It is a really good possibility that the plans you are trying to make may very well fall short of what Spirit has in mind for you. Rather than allowing fear to come up within you, open your heart and mind long enough to feel the peace that is gently reminding you that everything will be ok. You may not be able to coordinate everything as you'd wish it might be, but you can be sure that any planning that Spirit creates will go beyond your best expectations.

OCTOBER 11th

So What

When you put yourself down and constantly talk negatively about everything going on around you it can completely consume all of your time. Time is such a precious resource that we don't have much of in the first place, so do not waste it in a way that will not benefit you or anyone around you. It is also very insulting to the very one that created you. Couldn't you just this one time see yourself as God created you? What are you really accomplishing by beating yourself up about things that don't really matter? Do you think all this hatred you put on yourself will ever create a safe enough space to excel? So you've made mistakes. SO WHAT! Spirit doesn't make you pay for them over and over so why should you?

OCTOBER 12th

Time Is A Milestone

While some days seem so long, others speed by rather quickly. Before you know it, what was yesterday really wasn't yesterday but more like 20 years ago. It can also feel like no time has passed. Maybe you reacquaint with a friend after many years and you pick back up without missing a beat. It's as if you had never been apart. It is really important to take enough time to experience each day to its fullest. Time can be just a point of reference so that we can keep track of the milestones in our journey. It's a way of learning how to heal from our experiences. So whatever speed time seems to be traveling in your life, remember that you have the ability to maintain your own healthy pace.

OCTOBER 13th

No Judgement

It is very disappointing to see a person stand in judgment of everyone around them, all the while they are justifying their behavior as the way they think God has called them to be. They use the words of our bible stories as a sword by which to slay the actions and ideas of those they don't agree with. They hide behind a false interpretation of what was being said and refuse to acknowledge that perhaps they are doing the very things that they claim is wrong in the eyes of Spirit. What a gift they may have if they just looked at things the way God does and that is through the eyes of love. There is no judgment and there is definitely no slaying of another by the words of Spirit.

OCTOBER 14th

Possibilities Spirit Has Been Planning

There comes a time in our day-to-day life that we lose momentum in something that has fueled our actions for so long. We have spent so much time building an image of who we think we are, that we lose track of what it really is that inspires us to be more. Situations arise that from the outsiders view appear to make no logical sense what so ever. There are moments that you realize that your own life really doesn't even make sense to you. It s as if you are suspended between one thing and another, or perhaps you feel disconnected from the predictable way you have been known for all these years. Be open to the possibilities that Sprit has been planning for you. Inspiration is anything but predictable.

OCTOBER 15th

Position Your Heart

One of the most loving things you can do for those you love is to be understanding and respectful to them when conflicts arise. While on one hand you feel totally justified to scream and yell and argue your point, the other hand is reminding you that behaving in that way will only give you more of what you don't want and that is hurting each other. Regardless of who is right, the breakdown of communication out of anger does nothing but destroy the beauty that is crying out to be seen. When you step past yourself and position your heart in a place that can see where they are coming from, then you might even be able to see yourself in another light.

OCTOBER 16th

You Are Responsible

Instead of trying to make someone else the cause of all your pain, take back your power and accept responsibility for yourself and the part you have played. Is it possible that on some level you agreed to all these situations that you have experienced? While many people think that everything and everyone is out to get them, they fail to realize that all of these situations have been miraculous opportunities to grow into a stronger, healthier person. If you can stop focusing so much on the drama of all the details and look at the situation with a much broader way of thinking then you will come to understand that the only person responsible for your life is you, both the good parts and the bad ones.

OCTOBER 17th

Rely On Spirit

When it comes down to getting things done in your life, you really only rely on Spirit and yourself. You may think you are being loving by patiently waiting for someone to step up merely because they keep saying they are going to. While the other person may genuinely believe that their efforts show they are trying, and in fact they may be trying it may not be enough to take care of the needs of those depending on it. Many times we become resentful with others because we feel trapped and disappointed. This is when it is time to take a stand and step up in the ways that you can. The responsibility we take for our own choices may help us to love others and our self through the difficult times.

OCTOBER 18th

Living Your Dreams

The anticipation of living out your days in the ways you've been dreaming of can keep you motivated in ways you didn't realize you were capable of. For each day you allow the many distractions that come up to divert you from your goals, is just another day you are postponing the very things you have been working for. Set your mind to something and then back it up with your passion and commitment and before you know it, you will see results. Gently remind yourself that Spirit is guiding you in every step of your journey and with a partnership like that you will finally know that there can be heaven on earth.

OCTOBER 19th

Another Day To Celebrate

Every day you wake up is another day to celebrate all you have to be thankful for. You may not see things clearly or how they are unfolding exactly as they should be. People tend to punish themselves for all the things they think they are doing wrong. But is it really wrong? Regardless of the outcome you may be hoping for, everything that is said or done is very much part of the learning experience you are having. Perhaps leaning to not doubt yourself as you remain true to trying to express how you feel may be part of the lesson. Letting go of the need to beat yourself up will be the first step in trusting that Spirit is beside you through it all. Love yourself enough to trust that you deserve to be happy.

OCTOBER 20th

Trust Things To Simply Unfold

When you allow Spirit to enter your life and lead the way it is nothing less than amazing to watch how simply all your dreams fall into place. Situations and circumstances line up in ways that you never imagined. What you could hardly believe you deserved is happening right in front of your eyes, and while you may be nervous about what is yet to come you can trust that every moment has been lovingly planned to help you along your journey. Take comfort in allowing yourself to be present in every moment for however long it lasts and remember that it really is the will of God for you to be happy. The way you choose to accept that you deserve this is completely up to you. Spirit really does know exactly what you need so trust things to simply unfold.

OCTOBER 21st

What Are You Afraid Of?

It can be difficult remaining balanced when you are feeling insecure. Even though you know things will go as they will, it is easy to let your mind wander to places that keep you doubting all the positive things you know to be true about your circumstances. What is it that you are really afraid of? When you feel insecure and inadequate to another person in a situation it is time to gently remind yourself that your fears are not important and can work against all the beautiful things that are going on in your life. When you remember that Spirit will guide you through the scary parts you can also stop worrying that your worst fears will become what is true for you.

OCTOBER 22nd

Commit To Your Happiness

Much of our lives seem to be dictated by our schedules of things we have committed to do. Whether that is our job, our family or other things, we seldom schedule time to unwind and do things that are out of our daily routine. We find a false comfort in always knowing the plan, how and when we will do something. We also find ourselves frustrated when we have things we'd like to do but don't seem to have time to do them. Perhaps the frustration is a signal that you need to creatively find a way to do more of the things that are out of the ordinary for you. Look at what you have committed to and see if it includes your happiness.

OCTOBER 23rd

All Around Us

There are many ways our loved ones will communicate with us. It isn't really very different even with our loved ones who are no longer walking with us physically on this journey. Our loved ones are connected to us in Spirit and are as close to us as they ever were. Perhaps the words of a song will be a reminder of a time shared, or a phrase you need to hear at a specific moment. A memory can be triggered by any of our senses. Some situations may occur in our lives and it is so obvious that we are being spoken to. Other times we simply don't pay enough attention to realize that what we need to experience is right in front of us, that the support we need is all around us, guiding us along our path.

OCTOBER 24th

A True Friend

A true friend is one that is happy for you in your successes and provides you a shoulder to cry on when you're falling apart. They never try to tell you how to fix your problems or judge you for choosing differently than they would. They let you be yourself and they support you when it's obvious that you don't even really know who you are. A true friend understands that your life is "on the job training" for everyone involved. You can reach out to them anytime of the day and for any reason. In fact you can reach out for no reason at all. They will be honest with you even if you don't want to hear it, because they will stand by you as you work things out. A true friend is one who reflects the love of Spirit to you always.

OCTOBER 25th

Divine Timing

Sometimes what seems like a senseless delay may actually be a huge turning point in one's life. Something may be about to happen that will change how you feel or react to something going on around you. The events and circumstances on your journey happen in the most divine timing. Our timing is not always the same as God's timing. Perhaps our previous experiences have not yet provided certain tools or ways of being we need in order to reach our next step. So when you get frustrated with things remember that time is an important part of your growth and what may seem like a delay is really just a blessing from Spirit that is providing you with the time you need in order to be prepared for what is next to come.

OCTOBER 26th

Surrender To The Process

The process of transforming from one stage of life to another can be really simple or incredibly hard. The decision you make about how you choose to see the situation will make all the difference in the world. When we look to Spirit to guide us through our day things will fall into place and we will be able to focus on all the positive aspects of the beautiful transformation process. When our ego steps up to demand that things go differently, is when things become difficult. If we can surrender to the process and have enough faith to remember that the universe is supporting us to become what Spirit has designed us to be. Make the choice to appreciate the process and you will see how beautifully simple it can be.

OCTOBER 27th

You Are Not Alone

Sometimes it just takes hearing someone's voice to remind you that everything is good between you. When you spend time apart from the person you are in love with, the distance can be both a blessing and a curse. In one instance you miss them so much and in another you begin to worry about what they may or may not be doing. Sometimes their actions or words will trigger in you an old wound. Most of the time it really has nothing to do with them. Allow these feelings to come up and take advantage of your alone time to work through these hurts, knowing that you are not really alone.

OCTOBER 28th

Just Excuses

Being spontaneous in your life can keep you feeling alive and vibrant. Many times people will think things through to such a degree that they will not even do something at all. They will think of all the reasons that they can't or shouldn't do something. All the while they appear to be trying to justify the logic of why it is better to plan every detail instead of just deciding that it would be a great plan to have no plan and just do it. In reality all these so called reasons are just excuses. More excuses to stay stuck and resentful of all the opportunities that you let slip by. So have enough faith to live your life with the spontaneity of Spirit.

OCTOBER 29th

You Set The Goal

When you set a goal in your life that is extremely important to you, it will often require you to make some choices that will help you achieve it. We get busy in our daily life and often lose track of just what it will take to accomplish what we have set out to do. Sometimes situations in our life may leave us feeling so overwhelmed that we actually impede our own progress because we end up doing nothing at all. When you focus on what you are trying to achieve and hold yourself accountable for either the progress or lack thereof in doing what it takes to achieve it, nothing but yourself will stop you from reaching your dreams. Remember it is you who set the goal so it is you that will make all the difference.

OCTOBER 30th

Open Your Heart

When you allow your heart to open to the love of Spirit you are opening your heart to infinite possibilities. For Spirit is truly part of everything and everyone around you. When you choose to see the positive side of all things it becomes clear that love is involved. By putting your attention on all the things that scare you and building a protective wall around your heart it becomes very unhealthy and blocks the way for love to enter your heart. It's ok to recognize your fears and consider ways to work through them but it is not good for you to look right past all the good things and give all your time and energy to the negative things. Open your heart and your eyes will also open to love.

OCTOBER 31st

Time And Space

Giving another person their own space and time can prove to be one of the greatest gifts that you can extend to someone. When you feel rushed or awkward about a situation it is important to look at all the circumstances involved and see if the respect is being shown towards the space needed and time given for things to unfold as they will. When we try to rush an outcome we can push people away and not even realize that we are dishonoring the relationship by behaving in a way that is less than loving. For with genuine love comes the truest form of respect. Every time we extend this gift to another it returns to us in even a greater abundance. You must give out what you yourself would like to receive.

NOVEMBER 1st

The Discovery Stages

When you meet someone and fall in love the more time you spend with them the stronger the bond becomes. The relationship you have with yourself and Spirit is just like that. When you open your heart completely you discover that the more you allow yourself to love them and respect the journey you have embarked on the more you will learn about yourself. Often times it is the discovery stages of what the other person is passionate about, you discover the many aspects of the different dynamics that make your relationship to others so magical. Take the time to enjoy how Spirit is working in your life and feel the divine strength in these loving connections.

NOVEMBER 2nd

Called To Duty

Often times we are called to duty in a variety of ways. Spirit will speak to us letting us know the direction we should take. We feel a passion and dedication in our heart to step up and serve this divine calling. We feel a tugging at our heart; sometimes nothing seems to make sense. Part of us truly understands that we need to trust Spirit enough to walk through all the changes and fears that will come up for us when we decide to answer the call. The other part of us is desperately trying to cling to all the comforts we have become used to hiding behind. Surrendering to the journey ahead will be necessary in order to move forward. Be still and listen to the call and know that you will be serving Spirit. You will always be supported in your journey.

November 3rd

Being Rerouted

Many times it can be difficult to see the blessing in every situation. When something very simple seems to go a completely different direction it can be not only frustrating but unexplainable. While you spend a lot of your valuable time and energy trying to understand what is going on it simply adds to your stress level. An unexpected delay or detour may very well be the perfect path that you should be taking to get to the place that Spirit would have you go. Perhaps in the middle of a chaotic event you encounter a person that you were destined to meet, you may have a conversation with someone that changes the course of their life. Maybe someone brings you an experience that would not have happened any other way. So don't waste time and energy on being frustrated, focus on the value of being rerouted.

NOVEMBER 4th

A Sacred Blessing

It can be a constant process to figure out how to stay on course to working out your issues. While one experience may pull our attention in one direction it may just be another opportunity to get some healthy boundaries with those around you that will support your decision to stay on track. Being aware of what your issues are and how others may trigger things to come up is a very important step to confidently moving forward in your healing process. We tend to take things personal when perhaps we are just feeling raw and vulnerable in a situation. When we step back and look at things from a more objective point of view we will understand that our so-called issues really contain a sacred blessing that is calling us to be more.

NOVEMBER 5th

A New Way Of Being

When you have lived your life in a certain way, it can be scary to feel drawn to things that challenge you to live differently. For example if you have always been very independent it may be a new experience to be in a relationship that doesn't require you to do everything on your own. Many times we have behaved a particular way, and then when we feel called to change we aren't sure how to do it or where to start. We have perfected the art of remaining in situations that are safe. Many times we fool ourselves into thinking that the way we have been doing things is making us happy. And then it happens, we meet someone that is so completely different, yet so much the same that we finally step out enough to walk into a new way of being, a way we never even dreamed of.

NOVEMBER 6th

Respect The Path

One of the hardest things to do in life is watch your loved ones struggle. While we want to be supportive of what they may be going through, over extending our sympathy and concern can not only hinder their growth but it is also inappropriate for us to over step the role that we are intended to play. While others may be able to provide guidance and insight to what we are experiencing, they really don't have a true understanding of what lesson Spirit may be providing. The most loving thing we can do for the people we care about is to respect the fact that they are walking their own path and discovering how to live their life in the highest good for them. The hardest path may be the most productive, so keep in mind that no matter what happens Spirit will take care of you.

November 7th

Let Spirit Be Your Guide

Many times things will not go as planned. Other times things will flow perfectly, almost too good to be true. We get attached to outcomes and place expectations not only on ourselves but on the world around us. It is in these moments that we notice that what we are doing is setting ourselves up for disappointment. If you come to expect nothing then you will no longer feel the need to try and coordinate life to work in such a way that will always produce the results that you think you want. Maybe what you want is not really as good as what Spirit has planned for you. All the effort you spend on living in ways that may produce these outcomes could be spend enjoying something even better. All things flow naturally when you allow Spirit to guide you.

NOVEMBER 8th

Open To Your Options

Getting organized enough to feel like you've made any progress can often be a challenge. Most of the time we expect so much from ourselves that we become overwhelmed before we have even begun. The secret to seeing results is to be clear on the goal and then take baby steps. When you know where it is that you're going, each step no matter how small it is or how long it takes you to make it, is still one step closer to where you are trying to go. If you take some time to visualize the entire process and make a logical plan on the actions you will need to take and in what order you, will notice that things will fall into place without much effort. Being flexible about the specific process will also help you stay positive and focused, so if one step falls short, you can simply pause and try again. The best way to stay organized is really to be open to your options.

NOVEMBER 9th

A Different Way To Look At Success

If you are willing to do what it takes to be successful in your life, then you will understand that many times we must first fail. We may fail so many times and so badly that we have convinced our self that success is not possible. But what is failure really? Failure is simply nothing more than an attempt to do something in a way that did not work. It is also another opportunity to try something different. If you can learn to accept these many failures as another opportunity for success you will then realize that while you may have thought you were failing along the way it was really a different way to look at success.

November 10th

Painful Judgements

The judgments of others can often be so painful that we allow it to overtake our life. We constantly try to do things that we think will make others around us proud. We pretend to be something we are not in order to avoid being judged. Most of the time what we feel we are being judged for is the very same thing we judge about another. More often it is the exact thing we have been persecuting our self for. Rather than looking at how detrimental our behavior has become we simply decide to look at everyone else. When you really stop long enough to face the fears you have about judgments, you will see that the painful source has been you all along.

NOVEMBER 11th

Trust What You Are Feeling

Many times the actions of a person say one thing and the words that are being spoken say things differently. Rather than over analyze what you think is being communicated simply be open to what you are feeling rather than what you are thinking. On the deepest level between people you know in your heart what the true intentions of another are regardless of what they do or say. You also know that if Spirit is at the center of your life then you can trust that what you are feeling on this level is true. You can believe that no matter how things seem to be going everything will unfold into the divine experience that it is meant to be.

November 12th

A Very Lonely Place

As people we tend to build walls as a way of protecting our self from being hurt. Every time we feel wounded or rejected we add another brick, we thicken up the layer we have surrounded our heart with. Many times people will make a decision to turn off their feelings completely so that they won't have to endure the discomfort. We spend so much effort policing this fortress that we almost become pure stone. The wall is so strong that it has become indestructible. We finally realize that the inner strength we have will be the only hope we have for breaking out of a self inflicted prison. For the very wall we have erected to keep others out is the same wall that has trapped us inside of a very lonely place.

NOVEMBER 13th

In The Presence Of God

Close your eyes and imagine that you are sitting in the presence of God. How would that look? What would you say? How do you feel? Sit with this image for a few moments. Expand your thinking to a state of feeling. Visualize the setting you are in. Hear the sounds around you, notice the fragrances you smell. Absorb this amazing feeling and now that you are safe, as you let down your guard and experience what is usually unthinkable. Then you wonder why haven't I ever thought of this before? It has been available all along. Now breathe in the experience into your very center. Now open your eyes and everywhere you look you will realize that you are in the presence of God.

November 14th

A Reminder Of Others

When we meet other people sometimes they remind us of a combination of many others that have been a part of our life at some other point in our past. Whether it was a quality we were drawn to or repelled by it made a lasting impression. Now with this new meeting of another person we can fondly remember some of our past lessons. It is in these situations that we must be mindful to honor the person for who they are and not what they may remind us of. Interestingly enough they may be feeling the same things about you. You would want a chance to be who you are rather than a distorted opportunity to relive something that is not even relevant. Appreciate the gift of the reminder and openly accept what new gift they have brought to offer you.

NOVEMBER 15th

You Are Enough

Just because the people in your life don't communicate with you in depth about how they may feel about you doesn't mean that they are not feeling things and in communication with others about how they feel about you. While we may think we are not getting past some of the bricks in the walls of others doesn't mean that those bricks are not being removed. When you put yourself out there and expose you're most vulnerable parts it can be a defense mechanism to close down and be unclear in your communication with the other person. The fear of disappointing them or not being who you think they want can overwhelm you so much that you appear to be unauthentic. Trust Spirit and yourself to know that you are loved and you are enough.

November 16th

The Right Timing

When we feel disappointed about something it can be very easy to stop listening to what is going on. Our ego screams for how things should be going, while Spirit whispers that everything will work out perfectly as it should. It may not go as we had planned, but you can be sure that it will go how it needs to go. When we are in the emotion of feeling hurt or rejected we become defensive and unable to be open and loving to what is taking place. All we can see is that we are not getting something we truly think we want at that moment. Perhaps when we take some time for things to settle we will be able to see that it is far more important to stay open and loving so that in the right timing we will get exactly what spirit has planned for us.

NOVEMBER 17th

What Another Sees

While it can be very flattering how another person feels about you, it can also leave you feeling a little undeserving. Many times we do not have a clear view of how we show up in the world. Our idea of our self is clouded by our efforts to feel deserving. If we let go of all the false understandings we have of our self and truly acknowledge how another person may feel about us, we may be surprised to find out what an amazing person we truly are. If another person can see this in us, why do we refuse to see it in our self? So when someone thinks highly of you, be grateful for the compliment and accept that maybe they are here to show you who you truly are.

November 18th

The Endurance Of Time Spent

The dedication it takes to honor a dream you have, can push you to a whole new way of being. Times you may have just sat back and watched your life pass by may now be spent over compensating for time you feel you wasted. Perhaps you are disappointed with yourself for not making a stronger commitment to following through sooner. Maybe if you forgive yourself enough to be patient and loving you will be able to notice that the time you felt was wasted was really valuable time spent on gaining more experience that would ultimately help you on your journey to achieving all the dreams you have. The endurance of time spent along the way was part of the dedication whether you choose to see it that way or not.

NOVEMBER 19th

It Is Not Necessary To Separate Yourself

We struggle with others to feel special and important in their life. We wish to be shown that we are a priority to them, because they may make us feel like we are more to them than others that they love. Making yourself separate from others to validate the role you play in someone's life can actually be destructive. An old pattern may be emerging from something that happened in the past that hurt you. Perhaps your trust had been broken by the actions of others that you never expected. Remember that you are important to others and it is not necessary to separate yourself into a category you label better so that you will feel a sense of security. We are all unique in our own way.

November 20th

The Support Of A Parent

When you experience the loss of a parent it often leaves you feeling like the biggest part of your past has just vanished. The crazy and embarrassing stories you would cringe at every time they told a new person suddenly become the same stories you'd give anything to hear. You wish you had paid better attention to all the little silly details that make them want to tell them in the first place. A parent has a way of reminding you how important you are to the world around you. On days when you don't really fell like you make any difference at all a parent will be the one to show you what unwavering support is all about. When you feel lost and alone remember that you still have the support, not only of your earthly parents but also of your heavenly father.

NOVEMBER 21st

Nothing Personal

Taking something personal can be a recipe for disaster. Someone says something to you and you automatically take offense and become hurt and defensive. Rather than realize that perhaps there is more to the situation you begin to over analyze it and start putting up the walls. You start making decisions based on your misinterpretation of how you should best react. The tone in their voice or the selection of their words really has a lot more to do with where they are in the moment than it has to do with you. Remember to stay in a healthy communication with them as you work through your own insecurities, you will realize that everything is fine. There is no need to a defense when a war has not been waged. Nothing is ever personal unless you choose it to be.

November 22nd

Be Authentic

Sharing what you have learned along your journey with others can greatly enhance their experience in this life. Many times in the sharing process you will learn more about who you really are. When we connect with others it is an opportunity to notice what kind of emotions or feelings come up for us when we are around them. It is quite possible that some of our buttons may get pushed at the very same time we are triggering something in them. While each person may choose to deal with things in their own way, it is crucial to the relationship that they are able to share with each other where they are in the experience. Sometimes the fear of rejection can be so overwhelming that we hold back from being completely honest when we choose to share the parts of our self we have keep guarded. Trust yourself enough to be authentic.

NOVEMBER 23rd

Refocus

It's funny how you can feel so confident in one area of your life and almost have no clue at all in another area what is going on. Many times when we are in our comfort zone we take for granted that things will go positively for us when we stand in our true power. The areas in which we allow fear to take over leaves us feeling defeated and weak. Many times we actually make things more complicated than they ever need to be when we operate our lives from that space. People are attracted to a person that has confidence in who they are. When you feel yourself beginning to slip into this state it is important to pause long enough to refocus your attention to your inner strength. When you learn to spend more time in this area the other things will fall right into place and life will be much simpler.

NOVEMBER 24th

No Need To Worry

When you worry about things it is as if you are saying to the universe that you don't trust things to go as they should. It is a clear indication that you are attached to an outcome, otherwise you wouldn't really be concerned with how things will go. While it is completely understandable to have an idea of the things we would like to have happen in our lives, it can also be stressful to lose sight of the fact that many times the journey along the way to a desired location may take us on many twists and unexpected turns. Be open to the possibility that we can have an amazing outcome without the need to worry. Trust that no matter what happens along the way the universe is on your side. Now perhaps you should get out of your own way.

NOVEMBER 25th

A New Perspective

Looking at your life from a broader perspective can help us to realize that what you are experiencing is not as over whelming and complicated as you think. It is the labels and limitations you attach to the things going on in your life that leave you feeling discouraged. You can never solve a problem from the same level of thinking that is causing it to begin with. You must rise above your current way of thinking in order to clear out enough space to allow a new way of thinking to enter. We tend to do the same things over and over without ever trying another way. The bigger something appears to be simply gets smaller if you step back far enough to be objective. Trust that Spirit will be there to guide you to a new perspective.

NOVEMBER 26th

Strongly Standing Beneath

Just because we cannot see something does not mean it is not there. When the clouds cover the moon you don't stop believing it to be there. You just know that in this moment it is not visible from where you are. The things that you know deep in your heart to be true can remind you that whether or not you can see them doesn't mean when they are out of focus they have left you. Many times in our lives we lose sight of some of the most important things in our life, sometimes we even believe that they are gone because we can't see that they are strongly standing beneath all the cloud cover between us. The blessing that Spirit offers us is to remember that just as easily as we separate our self we can also get back to alignment with what is really true in our life.

NOVEMBER 27th

In All Things Be Grateful

To appreciate things for how they are can be a constant opportunity to be practicing gratitude. While we may be truly grateful for the many blessings in our life, we may get off course by allowing our self to think things are different than they really are. We may participate in situations that are clearly going one way but we stick around just in case they go the way we may secretly be hoping they will go. Just remember you know what you signed up for, so when the circumstances arrive that leave you feeling insecure, stop what you're doing and appreciate things for exactly how they really are. For when you live in the present moment you will not be disappointed with all the false expectations that you may not even be aware exist. In all things be grateful.

NOVEMBER 28th

The Beauty Within

People can be like a geode. From the outside they look just like any other rock. Often they appear to be rough and ordinary. It can be amazing to see what is inside when it is cracked open. The beauty of all that is contained within can often be hidden by the hard protective exterior. With every crack that is put into the hard outer covering a little bit more of what's inside is allowed to peek out. If you can be loving enough to realize the beauty we all have within, you will be able to see past what may seem plain and of no value. Many times in our life we will experience things that create huge cracks in our protective coverings. Often times we may even fell like we have been broken open so wide that we are completely exposed. Trust Spirit enough to allow the beauty that is within to come out for the world around you to see.

NOVEMBER 29th

Prisoners To Our Past

We each are responsible for our own happiness. The decisions and choices we make in our lives will determine the level of happiness we can achieve. When we blame others in our life for the things that make us unhappy we are not being truly honest with the part that we have played. When we are small children we trust that our caregivers will protect us, often to be disappointed when they do not. Perhaps something happened to hurt us and we refused to move past it, so we carried it right into our adulthood. Instead of looking at how these things have helped us grow, we use them as a crutch to justify our blame. When we take responsibilities for where we are now we can truly live a happier life that isn't keeping us prisoner to our past.

NOVEMBER 30th

Grow With Spirit

Often times we are called to do more than we have been doing and to be more than we have been being. When you listen to Spirit and choose to answer this call things can sometimes feel disorganize in the process. Part of you is in a state of limbo, unable to make any plans at all. You don't yet know the next step or where you are headed but you can hear the voice speaking to your heart. You know that everything will go according to the divine plan. You will know when to make a move because it will be very clear. The process of waiting and wondering can leave you feeling frustrated. Focus on the many wonderful possibilities that lie ahead for you. Things will unfold in your life just as a flower will bloom. You cannot rush the process, so nurture yourself as you grow with Spirit into what you are designed to be.

D ECEMBER 1st

Your Role Together

Expressing to someone how grateful you are for the role they play in your life can take great courage. In one moment you feel your heart aching in pain and in another you are bursting with joy. There is no consistent way of behaving when a person you love dearly is helping you grow. While you may feel a distance at times, remember that too is part of the plan. Don't frown upon the low points of a relationship because that is what makes the highlights so much sweeter. It is easy to be grateful for the good times, but it can be a big blessing if we can see the value in the hard times. In order to remain balanced you must experience both. Be courageous enough to share how you feel with those in your life for the role that you play together.

DECEMBER 2nd

The Natural Flow

When life seems to be going exceptionally well it can be a challenge to remain focused on staying in this state. The most common human response to a lot of situations is to behave in an old comfortable pattern, interacting with others in the same old ways we always have. When we open our heart truly to allow Spirit to lead us, we should also remember that the reason things are going so well is because we are in the natural flow of how things should be. We fall off track when we start doubting that we deserve to be so happy. We are so used to being disappointed that we almost demand to bring about the very things we do not want. Walk with Spirit and call forth all the things you want, for those are the things you deserve.

DECEMBER 3rd

A Divine Shoulder

So many people are unwilling to allow themselves to cry. We have been told as small children that crying means we are weak and that we just need to suck it up and deal with things. We grow up into adults and believe that we must show the world we are tough. Allowing others to see that we are vulnerable is not always the easiest thing to do. In fact we become so good at hiding it that when we finally allow our self to open up we can become quickly overwhelmed at how raw we truly feel. Crying is the healthiest way to release the pain you are carrying around in your heart. It takes a much stronger person to cry and be honest with how they feel than it does to keep acting like nothing is wrong. Opening your heart may bring some tears but just know that you have a divine shoulder to help you through.

D
ECEMBER 4th

Stop Expecting

When you stop expecting things from others you will also stop being disappointed. When you do things simply because you want to, without a desired result you will not be upset if you do not get the response you were hoping for. Maybe the response will actually be more than you were expecting. When that is the case it is a pleasant surprise. We don't always respond to others in ways that they are expecting but usually we are not intentionally trying to disappoint them by our actions. If you remain true to how you are feeling in both scenarios whether it is giving or receiving, then it will not be possible to be disappointed, if the intentions are pure. So honor the connection with others by being genuine in all your actions.

DECEMBER 5th

Spirit Drew Your Hearts Together

Life can bring relationships into your experience that show you how to find peace while learning about yourself and the endurance of your heart. Sometimes two people can be so connected yet in very different places when it comes to some of the matters of the heart. When God is at the center of your life you can endure anything that you may experience. It can be a great reminder that when you feel a heart connection with another, Spirit will safely guide you through the experience even when all your insecurities and doubts start coming up. Remaining true to your heart and the highest good of all will enable you to feel confident as the other person learns to trust Spirit to work in their life too. For Spirit is what drew your hearts together in the first place.

D ECEMBER 6th

Back To You

The day-to-day activities in our life will often present us with many opportunities to grow. When a frustrating situation arises you can choose how you will react, it can either be in a loving way or you can add your own level of drama. Usually adding drama will only make things worse and things may continue to spiral into an even nastier experience for everyone. Choosing to act out of love can definitely bring about a much more productive experience for all involved. This is not always the easiest route to take but it is always the most appropriate if you desire a reasonable outcome. You may not get the results that you would like, but you will most certainly gain many things from the other person. It also starts with respect and trust, so when you act out of love you are honoring those qualities in others and it will all come back to you.

DECEMBER 7th

Little Gestures

The little things we do for others often makes a much larger impact on them than the things we think are big. Things have become so busy in our daily routines that we don't always make the time to extend small gestures because we think that no one will notice anyway. If you think about it you will realize that sometimes we take those gestures for granted until they stop happening. Then you notice that those little gestures really do bring a smile to your day. So if you can appreciate them in your life it is a safe bet that others will too. Don't hesitate because you think that everything you do must be in a big way so that others will appreciate you. Being thoughtful in any way is a reflection of how we should all treat each other.

D ECEMBER 8th

Another New Beginning

When things change, don't think of it as an ending but as another new beginning. We often get caught up in how we think things should go. Many times when you take a step back to see how it is that you are showing up in a situation, making some changes can be the best way to improve who you are and what you have to offer to the experience. Many times we will get involved in relationships that call us to be more then we have been. Spirit guides us into surrendering to who we are truly meant to be. Honoring one's self and where you are in your development is the first step to creating the life that you deserve to have. Once you have learned to love yourself it will be easier to love the others in your life. Listen to your heart and know that you are being guided to another new beginning.

D ECEMBER 9th

The Heart Is Gods Way

When you decide to follow what you are feeling in your heart, you can also trust that Spirit is guiding you gently into a beautiful experience. The pace in which we walk our path can often times feel like we will never arrive at the goal we are working towards. The true lesson of our journey is not in the destination we are striving to reach but in the path we travel to get there. We each have things in our life that we need to tend to in order to be in a place that we can walk our path with not only integrity but confidence in our self and our faith in Spirit to know that we truly do make a difference in this world. The heart is God's way of speaking to us to let us know how much we are truly loved.

D ECEMBER 10th

Be On Course

Getting on track with your life may require some self-evaluation. Perhaps you have been thinking that the way you have been living is the only choice you have. Maybe you have even convinced yourself that you are happy. The situations in your life may be just another result of settling for something that is better than what you have had. But it is as good as what you truly want? The choices and decisions we have made along our journey have brought us to where we are now, but it this where we are trying to go? Is this the person we were designed to be? If you are honest with yourself you can recognize that while many things in your life are wonderful perhaps you can align with Spirit and finally be on course to all that you were created to be.

D ECEMBER 11th

Yesterday, Today, Tomorrow

Spirit can be seen in everything around you, in the most complicated situation or the simplest idea. Take for example the flower known as the yesterday, today and tomorrow plant, it blooms in the way it was created by Spirit and it starts out as a beautiful purple flower, changes to a lighter purple and then becomes white. When you look at this plant each flower is at a different stage in the process, but viewed together as one it is breathtaking. People are also like that, each at their own stage in the development process, just being who they were created to be. We are always evolving to be more of who we are designed to be, so remember to honor the process and see the beauty in everyone along the way, because together we are all truly beautiful.

DECEMBER 12th

Like A Brownie

When you decide to make brownies there is a process that you must follow. First you need to gather all the ingredients that will create a brownie, then you combine the appropriate things together. You add the eggs, the oil, the brownie mix and whatever else is needed to make the dessert in the way you desire it. Once the mixture is put into the appropriate pan it is then time to put it into the oven where it will transform from a mix into what you know as a brownie. When you complete the process there are many ways to serve and enjoy your efforts. While you cannot see the original form of each and every ingredient that made up the brownie, you know that everything was needed in order to make things possible. Life is very much like this, everything is a necessary ingredient that will yield a beautiful life that you can share and serve to others.

DECEMBER 13th

On The Right Track

What may look like a baby step to others may actually be a huge step for the person making it. Everyone on this journey is developing at a different pace. We are each evolving at the perfect speed. In the big scheme of things there is certainly a divine timing to everything that happens. Our life will unfold in a sequence of events that fit together perfectly even though we may not realize this. When we open our heart to Spirit and become present in the moment we will no longer feel overwhelmed with where we think we need to be on our path. For when we start trying to push our self faster than we need to go we will only impede our progress. Just know that you are on the right track.

DECEMBER 14th

Where You Are Needed

Many times we get so focused on certain things in our life that we tend to over look other areas in our lives that also need attention. We take people for granted that have always been there for us and we forget that maybe they need us to be present with them and things that they may be going through. Making the time to nurture the people and relationships in your life will be worth the effort. Things can change very quickly and what you depend on to be there can be gone in an instant. Trust Spirit to guide you to where you are needed. When plans fall through it may simply be a way to put you on a different track, a reminder that there are other people that can help you remember who you truly are.

D ECEMBER 15th

The Journey Of Self-discovery

In order to experience who you truly are you must also have had to experience who you are not. We constantly evolve into being a better person. We experience things in life that show us how to love. Many times it is in the crying out of our heart that we discover that the only way to find it is to feel the absence of it. We may take things for granted until something happens in our life to remind us how valuable every moment is. Every stage of your life is a crucial part of becoming the person you were designed to be. Be loving towards yourself and others when you notice that perhaps you are being the person you are not, for in every moment Spirit is guiding us to discover all the many wonders of our journey of self-discovery.

DECEMBER 16th

The Freedom Of Choice

People make choices for many different reasons. While others may not understand why a person may choose one way over another, in time everyone will come to understand that every choice made is part of the divine lesson that is playing out. Perhaps you would have chosen differently, but in any case God is speaking to them in the decisions that they must make. Our choices do not have to make sense to anyone nor do they need to make sense to us. What does need to be honored is the fact that one of the greatest gifts we have been given is to have the freedom to make our own choices. While some decisions we make may hurt us or others we can remember that it was all how it should be. So rather than focus on the hurt, look past it to see all of the good that also came from those choices.

DECEMBER 17th

Radiate The Beauty

When you show up in this world as you were truly created to be, the impact you have on the world around you can simply be amazing. When you share who you are with others it can inspire them to be more than they have allowed themselves to be. The example that you set when you are coming from a place of love can remind others that what we all truly want is to be loved without conditions or limits. When we honor Spirit we begin to understand how that kind of love feels. Once we experience that kind of love it is easy to share it with others. For when we remove the blocks to love we can begin to experience a deeper love that will enhance the quality of our life. We stand representing the God we serve and we radiate the beauty to the entire world around us.

DECEMBER 18th

Quick To Protect

When we pray to be the hollow bone that Spirit will work through to reach those around us, we may hesitate because we get caught up in the ways we behave as humans. We must take a step back and remember that we need to behave in the ways of our higher self. For our higher self is confident in all tasks that Spirit may have us participate in. The human part of us is quick to protect ourselves from being hurt or in an uncomfortable position. Perhaps what is needed for the growth of everyone is a difficult situation that will enable the ability to move beyond where they are. Trust that when you surrender completely to Spirit you are safe in any situation especially the scary ones.

DECEMBER 19th

The Belief Of Others

While we may feel we are open and respectful to the beliefs of others, we need to examine in our self some of the things that people may do that we do not relate to. Is it because we do not understand, or is it because we do not agree? Usually it is a little bit of both. If we truly understood what other people believed then we would be able to relate to it on some level. Perhaps the ideas and actions that repel us are not because we don't agree but that someone in our past did not respect us enough and tried to forcefully place their views and beliefs on us by making us feel small and unworthy because we did not feel the way they did. Knowing that behaving in a way less than loving pushed us away in the first place can also be the gift that will allow us to find peace within our self. Then we will be able to truly respect others and their beliefs.

DECEMBER 20th

Reflections Of Our Self

What is it that draws you to another person? Is it the way they carry themselves? Or maybe there is something about them that you find intriguing. In any case we are all drawn to each other so that we may learn more about who we really are. When we meet a new person or simply spend more time with someone we already know we have the opportunity to share our thoughts and feelings. We also have the opportunity to observe how they react or respond to our connection during our interaction. If we honor the other person for who they are then we will be able to appreciate them for who they show up as in this world. We will meet many different kinds of people but ultimately they are really just reflections of our self.

DECEMBER 21st

Struggling For Control

Sometimes when conflict arises it can be clear that both sides are struggling for control. Rather than trying to find a peaceful compromise both parties fight to be right. Often times it may be necessary to agree to disagree. When someone feels passionate about their point of view they often lose track of why they are really disagreeing with the other person. When you step back enough to look at the bigger picture you will see that there really isn't a good reason to be fighting over something that is silly. Try to see things from the other person's point of view and pause long enough to really listen to what they are saying. Would giving in or deciding that maybe you are both right in your own way be so difficult if in the end it helped to strengthen the relationship?

D ECEMBER 22nd

Seeking Changes

Most of the time when a person has difficulties in their life it usually stems from a way of thinking. The way we view our problems is very relevant to the thinking we have that could be the key to making the necessary changes that will fix the very issues we think we are having. What are the things in your life that you would like to change? If someone else came to you and needed advice on the situations that match your situations you would have the ability to offer suggestions on how they may be able to make some improvements to their life. Isn't it interesting that you can be the supportive friend to another and give fabulous feedback yet you can't apply this simple logic to your own life. Be the friend to yourself first and you will see that the changes you seek are seeking you.

D ECEMBER 23rd

Unspoken Communication

There is an unspoken communication that occurs between all living things. Take for example household pets; they don't have voices that they can use to tell you what they need. Their actions and body language can speak just as loudly as any words that could be spoken. They have the ability to interact with the family as well as each other. While the mannerisms of a cat are quite different than that of a dog it is quite natural for them to be able to co-exist and even develop a very close connection. Unspoken communication is a vital part of any relationship because many times we are unable to choose words with meanings that can express what we may be trying to say. Listening from your heart works better than just using your ears.

DECEMBER 24th

In Anticipation

In the anticipation of Christmas day we can get caught up in ways that on the surface may appear to reflect what the holiday represents but on another level it is merely a superficial outcome to how we think we should behave. We prepare our homes in festive décor; we bring out our best china to serve all the foods that we traditionally eat in celebration of the upcoming day. The gifts are wrapped and under the tree waiting for our loved ones to open them. We almost exhaust our self in preparations that may or may not even be appreciated by those we are hoping to serve. Step back and look at the beautiful gestures you are creating and remember who you are honoring on the upcoming day and you will know in your heart that all your efforts are genuinely appreciated.

DECEMBER 25th

A True Gift Can't Be Wrapped

In today's society the real reason for this season has been completely overlooked. People rush around trying to buy gifts for the people in their lives. Some buy things out of obligation while others purchase things with resentment. Money is often spent on things that are not needed or even wanted by some as a way of saying they are important to you. The things of most value are not available in a store and should not be limited to just one day. The things that a person truly needs and wants can't be wrapped with paper or taken back for a refund. When we are expected to buy things for others to show our love it can cause unnecessary hurt. For the value of a true gift has no monetary measure that could ever compare. Love your family and friends this day to honor the true meaning of the season.

DECEMBER 26th

Seek The Beauty

As we prepare to move in to a new year we can take with us all the beautiful lessons that we have had the chance to experience. The opportunities to spend time with family and friends have added many more memories to the journey we are on. While our days may have also been filled with tragedy and sadness we can look back and find the comfort that was as much present with us in those moments as it was in the easy ones. Knowing that we are truly supported in every step we take can help us find comfort as we grow with Spirit. What may be looked at as a positive experience can remind you that when you trust completely things will work out as they should. We hardly ever doubt our faith when things go well, it is in the difficult times that we need to seek the beauty in the situation and remain diligent in our faith.

DECEMBER 27th

Relax And Enjoy

The completion of a project you have been working on cannot only bring up excitement but it can also present a little bit of fear. The ability to reach a goal can be the most amazing feeling. In some respects it feels almost the same as any other moment because you know that there is much more still to come. Trusting Spirit to guide you on to the next step is very crucial at this moment because it would be very easy to over think things that you may need to do next but have absolutely no idea how to do it. Remember that all Spirit ever asks us to do is be clear and show up. The details will all work out in the divine way and timing. The fun is just beginning so relax and enjoy the experience that Spirit will be bringing you and know that you deserve it.

DECEMBER 28th

Many Paths

There are many pathways that lead to Spirit. Just as there are many types of people, God speaks to each and everyone in the ways they understand. There are many different religions and spiritual practices. For many centuries people have fought each other in an attempt to prove that the way they believe is the correct way. Rather than respecting all the ways in which God speaks to his children people stand in judgment of what they believe to be true. What one person identifies with may not speak to the heart of another; therefore other ways need to be sought out. The bottom line regardless of the path you choose is to develop a relationship that is meaningful to you with Spirit in a way that you understand and are inspired by so that you will become all you were created to be.

D ECEMBER 29th

Be Willing

We must each find our own way to deal with the experiences and hardships we have in our life. When something painful happens in our life we can easily shut down on many levels. We bottle up all our feelings and refuse to talk to anyone about how we are feeling. We operate in our day to day life and pretend that everything is fine and that we don't need anyone to talk to. Oddly enough we can only pretend for so long and then everything we do seems to be out of anger or frustration. Things that would normally not bother us can cause us to behave in an irrational outburst. This outburst is always justified to us and the cause is everyone but us. At some point we must hit the bottom so that we will finally raise our eyes enough to see that we do need something to help us up. We must be willing.

DECEMBER 30th

Something New

The anticipation of something new can often leave us feeling overwhelmed and very excited. On the other hand it can also bring up great fear. We imagine all the possibilities that will arrive with these experiences. Approaching something new with joy and excitement is exactly what Spirit wants us to do. For when we allow our heads to control things we often get in the way of what Spirit is bringing. We allow our so called logic to team up with the ego and before you know it we have not only covered over the joy we have also created even more obstacles and blocks that stand in the way of what these new experiences will bring and that is an opportunity to learn more about love.

DECEMBER 31st

Learning To Balance

Our experiences in life can be very unpredictable. As one new journey comes to an end another one begins. We reflect back on the previous year and all its many opportunities we had to learn and we are then able to see just how closely Spirit has been with us for each and every step. The challenges of our last year were filled with both heart aching moments of pain and breath taking moments of joy. Learning to balance our mind and hearts can be tricky when in one moment we are on the highest cloud and the next we have been knocked straight to the ground. It is in these moments that we must remember that Spirit is right beside us and that something good truly does come from every moment as our soul remembers how to love.

Index

June 1 Be Proactive Instead Of Reactive
June 2 Embrace The Differences
June 3 Teaching You To Grow
June 4 It Will All Work Out Just As It Should
June 5 Endless Possibilities
June 6 Arrive In Your Glory
June 7 The Quality Of Our Days
June 8 Respect Others For The Part They Have Played
June 9 Accept The Life You Are Meant To Have
June 10 Finding The Balance
June 11 Go Forward In Your Day
June 12 We All Make A Difference
June 13 Genuine In Your Intentions
June 14 Space To Experience The Results
June 15 Something Bigger
June 16 Give Yourself Permission
June 17 The State Of Pure Innocent Love
June 18 Spirit Will Bring You Through
June 19 Focus On The Good
June 20 Honor And Respect Yourself
June 21 Sing Your Song
June 22 Free To Go
June 23 Searching For What Is Within You
June 24 Not Our Place To Interfere
June 25 Love Of Spirit In The Truest Sense
June 26 A Divine Experience To Expand Your Heart

June 27 Enjoy Where You Are
June 28 Vital Connections
June 29 The Universe Has Lined Up Your Dreams
June 30 Grateful To Feel Something
July 1 A Painful Separation
July 2 The Same Lesson
July 3 Everything Really Does Happen For A Reason
July 4 Happy Independence Day
July 5 A Step Closer To Moving Past Your Fear
July 6 Do What Your Designed To Do
July 7 No Need To Defend
July 8 See Things As They Are
July 9 Start By Changing How You Look At You
July 10 Simply Because You Are You
July 11 Attachment And Connection
July 12 Who We Are
July 13 Passion To Create
July 14 Feel Comfort In The Unknown
July 15 Remain Centered
July 16 Choosing To Walk Through Our Lesson
July 17 Healing With Every Breath
July 18 Spirit Working In You As You
July 19 What Spirit Designed Friendship To Be
July 20 More In Store For You
July 21 Innocence Of A Baby
July 22 Remembering Who We Are

CPSIA information can be obtained at www.ICGtesting.com
Printed in the USA
LVOW010148031011

248734LV00001B/1/P